Finding Your Perfect Partner

The Foolproof Dating, Rating and Mating System

by

Marsha Wayne, MACP, MBA

authorHOUSE

1663 LIBERTY DRIVE, SUITE 200
BLOOMINGTON, INDIANA 47403
(800) 839-8640
www.authorhouse.com

First published by AuthorHouse 08/12/04

ISBN: 1-4184-2613-X (e)
ISBN: 1-4184-2614-8 (sc)

Printed in the United States of America
Bloomington, Indiana

This book is printed on acid-free paper.

I dedicate this book to my husband of over twenty years, my most special and last true love.

And to my four daughters, one son, one son-in-law, three potential sons-in-law, my nieces and nephews and their families, and my two granddaughters.

May they always have love.

Contents

Why This Book?

According to recent 2000 census data,

- There are more single people today than ever, 82 million in the United States, over 40% of the adult population.
- The marriage rate is decreasing and is at its lowest rate in 30 years.
- Of those who do marry, 40 to 60% will be divorced in 15 years or less.

The statistics show that Americans are marrying less, are more unhappy when they do, and have a 50-50 chance of getting divorced.

Clearly what we're doing is not working. We're spending a lot of time trying to date the wrong person or just anyone at all! We're becoming demoralized about our ability to ever attract the right person. And we're hooking into dead-end relationships.

Or, if we are out there "successfully" dating, we're apt to choose someone because they look nice, have a few social charms and are at the right time in their life to consider commitment. Soon, we lose ourselves to romance, lust and sexual attraction; decide to get married; and wake up 18 months later, realizing that we don't have a clue about the person we're with.

How I wish this book had been available when I was in the dating and mating stage! I struggled with finding the perfect mate for me. Fortunately, I was lucky enough to get it right the first time. And as in the Robert Frost poem, *The Road Not Taken*, "that has made all the difference." My life is completely different in a wonderful way because of the man I married.

But luck had a lot to do with it. Today, I can offer you skills and techniques that bring you a lot more certainty of success than luck ever could.

So why do I, a happily, long-married woman, think I know anything about finding lasting love? Three things.

First of all, what makes relationships work has been a long-time interest of mine. I've seen so many friends and relatives fail at finding the right person. I've witnessed all the pain and heartbreak they went through, and then seen them make the same mistakes all over again. There has to be a better way, I thought. And so I began questioning why some relationships worked and some didn't.

Secondly, because of my interest, I've made it a point to read what was available on finding soul mates and making relationships work. I also chose to practice couples counseling. I saw first-hand how hard it is to retrieve a terrible relationship- in fact, the statistics show that only one out of eight marriages will be saved through marriage counseling. I'm convinced that if we took more time and trouble in the selection process, the divorce rate would go down.

Third, through my reading and my work, I began to see patterns of what worked and what didn't. I found that problems usually start with whom we choose, which may be caused by circumstances and beliefs that we're not even aware of, and then, if unchecked, continue on to inevitable failure.

As I studied and worked with singles looking for love and couples in trouble, I began to devise a different system: if you pick the right person for the right reasons, and take it slowly, and learn to communicate and respect each other, then your chances of succeeding are dramatically increased.

Building on my interest, my experience, and my research, I have written this book in the hope that you, gentle reader, will use it to overcome the obstacles and detours in the path, and take the road not yet taken, the road to finding your true love.

Marsha Wayne

Two roads diverged in a wood and I,
I took the one less traveled by,
And that has made all the difference.
Robert Frost

Introduction

What is my goal in writing this book? It is to help my readers find Love. Perfect Love. Love that lasts. That is sexy, fun, nurturing, and abundant. What do people want more than anything else? Love. What seems the hardest thing to find? Love.

Is there a scientific, proven way to find love? No. I can't promise100% results. But my seminar participants and clients have found that my approach works.

Why?

Because it provides **DATING** skills on:
- Where to look for a positive relationship
- How to have a confident, no-fail attitude
- How to be irresistibly attractive

Because it provides **RATING** tools to help:
- Determine the ideal match for you
- Avoid someone who rings your bells but is completely wrong for you
- Stop making decisions with your heart and not your head

Because it provides **MATING** wisdom on:
- Knowing when to hold and when to fold 'em
- How to resolve couple's conflict

- How to build relationship esteem
- How to get the perfect partner to the altar

Magic may occur when you find your true love, but <u>finding</u> true love in **this** book is the result of a systematic and purposeful approach. I see helping you find love as similar to leading Dorothy to the Land of Oz. First, I'll construct the yellow brick road for you to follow so that you arrive at your destination of committed love with the perfect partner. (And aren't sidetracked by all the monkeys and munchkins along the way.) Then I'll take the role of Glinda, the Good Witch of the North, to offer you smiling and loving encouragement. I'll supply the companions of brains, courage and heart embodied by the scarecrow, lion and tinman, so you won't grow lonely and disheartened on your journey.

And then, I'll give you help in slaying the demons like the Wicked Witch of the West that keep you from reaching your goal. Finally, I'll make sure you reach the Magic Kingdom of Oz where you'll find that all the magic and wizardry comes from knowledge that's already within you. (No? Then I'll supply some of that knowledge, too.)

Or, if you aren't fans of Dorothy, imagine finding love as similar to landing a spaceship on the moon. Before you can achieve lift-off, you need to construct a craft that is suitable for the voyage, that can lift-off, climb and travel through different atmospheres in a graceful, strong and undaunted manner. After launch, the spacecraft you create must withstand the journey unharmed, gliding past all unknown obstacles and foreign bodies. And—the purpose in the first place—it must reach its target, landing at its destination with precision and safety. I will show you how to create a safe and trouble-free way to reach your destination of perfect love.

The purpose of this book is also to help my friends and readers from settling on the NOT perfect partner, to save them the months to years of wasted time, frustration, uncertainty, loss of self-esteem and heartache that comes from picking the wrong person.

Put more strategically, the purpose of this book is to help you create a "new you," a person that is ready for and capable of finding love, mapping and outfitting you for the journey and strengthening you in every way possible so that you can reach your target and find your ultimate destination of happiness and true love, correcting at some points in midcourse perhaps, but never faltering along the way. We begin the journey at . . .

The giving of love is an education in itself.
Eleanor Roosevelt

Chapter One – Pre-Dating

The Pre-Dating stage begins when you start to read this book and continues until you have:

- Assimilated an optimistic mental attitude toward finding love
- Figured out what has gone wrong in the past
- Made any corrections to your behavior that are necessary to be in a successful relationship
- Developed the physical appearance that you like
- Made your life bounteous
- Closed all old doors and
- Put boundaries and standards in place to protect yourself.

This is about what you do <u>before</u> you start the journey—i.e., getting ready and clearing the way to hone in on the perfect partner. First of all,

Examine your Beliefs
Do you believe that

To love oneself is the beginning of a lifelong romance.
Oscar Wilde

- There is something wrong with you because you are not in a relationship?
- There are no compatible partners out there?
- You are too picky?
- You will be alone for the rest of your life?

The truth is:
- There **are** healthy, single, available, vibrant people of both sexes out there
- You **can** learn to find and attract them
- There is no such thing as being too picky- well, maybe there is, but we'll discuss that later
- You do not have to be alone for the rest of your life
- You do not have to wait years for the right person to show up
- You do not have to "settle"
- There are **skills** and **behaviors** that can make you attract potential partners

I will teach you the skills and behavior. It's easier than you think. And No, you don't have to completely change who you are.

But first, you have to **believe**. Believe that you have the capacity within yourself to be a loving, caring, dynamic partner. Believe that love **will** happen to you.

At this point in *Peter Pan*, Tinker Bell would step out and ask if you believe in fairies. Here is your time to state clearly and boldly, **"I do believe that I can and I will find love with the perfect partner."**

Having convinced yourself that there are abundant numbers of partners out there, the next step you must take in order to be successful at dating is to come "out in the open" and make finding the right partner . . .

A Project.

You need to go on Partner-Project status. It's not just going to happen. If you're looking for love in all the wrong places, you're not going to find it. If you keep on doing what you've always done, you'll keep on having what you've always had.

So ask yourself:

- Do I really want to have a relationship right now?
- Am I willing to tell my friends, family and co-workers that I'm looking for my true love?
- And if I can't do that, why can't I?

Did you know that being ashamed is the #1 factor that sabotages people's dreams of finding a partner? Now is the time to change your thinking and direction. If you just sit at home and do nothing, waiting for Prince Charming or Cindy Crawford to knock on your door, nothing will happen. To change your life you must **take action**.

Fact: Fifty percent of singles still meet other singles through friends and family. Therefore, **you're** going to have to let them know you're looking.

Not choosing is a choice. Is it yours? Getting into action and really managing your life means that you stop living in **Re**-action and start becoming **Pro**-active.

You are starting a new project . . . a Partner Project!

Like any other project you need to
1. Commit to putting the time into making it succeed
2. Prioritize it above other activities

3. Give it thought, time and energy every day

Are you ready to make finding the significant person in your life, the person you want to spend the rest of your life with, the person who warms your heart and excites your mind and thrills your body a commitment, a priority, and a project that you will devote your best to every day?

Then say **"Yes! I am so ready!"**

And let's begin . . .

Working on Yourself

Stage 1 of the Partnership Project–The Mental Part
Here's where we examine what messages you're giving yourself and what faulty thinking you're using that's keeping you stuck.

The Six Steps to Free Yourself from Old Patterns

1. Ask yourself: "What has been holding me back?"
2. Free yourself from the stigmas of shame, embarrassment and fear of looking needy or desperate.
3. Resolve the need to be perfect.
4. Be aware of other's availability.
5. Admit that you are afraid of something . . . intimacy, rejection and/or failure.
6. Analyze your past and then let go of it.

Let's examine these Six Steps more thoroughly.

1. Ask yourself: "What has been holding me back?"

Old fears? Myths? A negative, gremlin voice inside your head? The voice that might be saying, "I'm too fat," "No one will be interested in me," "I don't make enough money." For example: someone may have violated your trust. You vow, "I'm never going to let anyone get that close again. I'm never going to go through that humiliation, pain, and loss again!" At the same time, you really yearn for love, and you know that to feel love you're going to have to get close to someone again.

What to do? You have to decide. Is it more important to you to never get hurt again or to find love? I believe my method will help you get close without getting hurt and will teach you how to protect yourself from premature intimacy. But there's still a risk. Decide now if you're willing to take it.

Or are you waiting for that wonderful person to just appear? Are you a Cinderella-in-waiting? Don't depend on the stars; make your own fate.

2. Free yourself from the stigmas of shame and embarrassment or the fear of looking needy and desperate.

If you are not dating because you are embarrassed or ashamed of something about yourself or your life, then make an appointment with a therapist to work through it. If that isn't possible, talk with a close confidant or read a book on the subject. Deal with whatever is causing your embarrassment or shame. Don't let these feelings keep holding you back. Often, in the light of day, they are not that important, especially to someone else.

And to tell someone that you are looking for a partner or someone to just go out with doesn't mean you're needy. It means you're in-between. We've all been there. And one of the best ways to find someone new is to ask acquaintances to set you up.

3. Resolve your need to be perfect.

If you postpone living until you are perfect, the chances are that you will never start having any fun, let alone meet someone. Think of your life as a work in progress and start living in the Now. Don't let life pass you by. Be "Good Enough," not perfect.

4. Be aware of your and others' availability.

Do you continually pick unavailable people?

What are situations that make people unavailable to another person? There is emotional unavailability and situational unavailability.

Emotional unavailability

When someone is fresh out of a marriage or important relationship their emotions are still raw. They will probably be grieving and may be carrying anger and guilt that must be resolved before they are able to give freely to another person.

Situational unavailability
  a. Someone in his/her first year of sobriety is encouraged to stay unattached romantically.
  b. Someone with an exciting, exacting new job is probably not going to have the time, energy, and/or resources to commit to a relationship at this time. In today's world, the job commitment comes first.

In the eyes of a lover pockmarks are dimples.
Japanese proverb

5. Admit that you are afraid of something... intimacy, rejection and/or failure

Intimacy. When I say intimacy I'm not speaking of physical intimacy. I'm talking about emotional intimacy, the ability to open up and really let someone know who you are, including your fears, feelings and vulnerabilities.

Rejection. You may give in to your fear of being rejected because it is painful. It is also something that everyone has experienced. You can't get through this life without some type of rejection. So, the question is: Are you going to allow fear of rejection stop you? Or can you learn to accept a certain amount of rejection, whomever you are, as part of the cost of entering the game? And then, can you figure out how to take care of yourself, hopefully, **before** it happens and, if necessary, **after** it happens to you?

This is where I can help you. I'll teach you how to:

- Go slow
- Be cautious
- Watch for red flags and
- Not give your heart away too soon.

Failure. Many people fear failure. Men fear that they won't be able to provide financial and/or emotional support or they won't be able to stay faithful. Both sexes fear they won't be able to live up to their partner's expectations.

If your parents are divorced, you may have seen failure and pain. And you may unwittingly sabotage a relationship because of fear of failure. You may think, "I don't deserve this person. They're too good for me.

7

Sooner or later, they'll realize that. So I better ruin the relationship first before it is ruined for me."

The first step in dealing with fear is to be aware that you have it. The second step is to analyze whether it's a rational or irrational fear. If it's a rational fear, what can you do to protect yourself against it? List the ways you can take care of yourself. [I'll also provide hints as we go along.]

I will protect myself from a rational fear by _____

_____.

If it's an irrational fear, write down exactly what the fear is. _____.

I know it's irrational but my fear is _____

_____.

Now state the reasons that the fear is irrational. *The evidence that this fear is irrational is that*

    1. _____
    2. _____
    3. _____
    4. _____

Make an index card of this evidence to remind yourself that the fear is not realistic when you start going to that place.

6. Analyze and then let go of your past.

Does your past keep you from moving forward?

Ask yourself what you learned from your past relationships. Why did they end? It has to be you picked the wrong person, you did something wrong, or circumstances intervened.

You'll notice that I'm a big believer in taking responsibility for your own life and not blaming it on the other person. This actually gives you more leeway because it's certainly easier to change yourself than someone else!

So go back and re-examine every significant relationship you've had since you were sixteen. List them chronologically.

Name	Age	My fault	Their fault	Circumstance
1.				
2.				
3.				
4.				
5.				
6.				
7.				
8.				
9.				
10.				

Is there a pattern here? Name it in 10 words or less.

My relationships have not lasted because

_____.

By doing this exercise you will diminish the chances of making the same mistakes again. It's not failure; it's feedback.

You absolutely must forgive yourself for actions for which you are embarrassed, ashamed or regretful. (Re-read point #2.) Try to understand the circumstances that made you behave the way you did. In most cases, your behavior will be perfectly understandable. Let go and move on.

Attempt to forgive the other person as well. Sometimes this is more difficult than forgiving yourself because the pain may be lingering. As soon as you begin to forgive, however, it gets easier. Remember that you're not forgiving them for their sake but for your own, so that you can move ahead rather than be brought back to a negative place.

Another way to let go of your past is to write letters to people with whom you are not emotionally finished. This helps to relieve the hurt and/or anger. Don't mail the letters, but use them as a method to get all your anger, frustration and negative feelings **out!** Or talk with a close confidant about your feelings, telling and re-telling your story as many times as needed. The objective here is to free yourself mentally to move on and start searching for your true love.

Now that you've read the Six Steps, complete the assessment below to be sure you are clear on what has held you back.

Assessing your progress

Circle the items that apply to you.

1. I have shame, embarrassment and/or fear about
   _____.

2. I feel the need to be perfect in the following areas:
   _____.

3. I pick unavailable people like _____

4. I am afraid of intimacy, rejection and/or failure.

5. I have not yet let go of my past. I have unresolved issues that are holding me back.

Stage 2 of the Partnership Project: Taking Action

If you have boldly stated your intention to find the Perfect Partner, and if you have cleared the mental obstacles from the path, it is time for **Action**. Here are the first seven steps:

1. Be a really great catch!

Water seeks its own level. Fantastic people marry fantastic people. Recognize that you must have your own great life first before meeting someone else who has a great life. Don't tell yourself that you need another person to make your life great or happy. You have **you**!

But what makes a great life? It's the one that makes **you** happy. Authentically happy. If you have to play games or twist into a pretzel so someone else will approve of you, then you **lose** you. Gary Zukov, in *Seat of the Soul* writes, "When the personality merges with the soul's needs then you are living an authentic life." It is much easier to be and act **yourself** than try to be what **others** want you to be. Instead of being an "other-people pleaser" become a "self-pleaser."

Part of being a really great catch involves being responsible and available. Many behaviors will automatically ruin any relationship. Examples are raging, workaholism, depression, drug use, alcoholism, and sexual addiction.

These are all areas that can be changed, modified, or controlled. Would you want to enter a new relationship and deal with this kind of chronic problem? No! Nor does anyone else. Solve your personal problems and learn to control outrageous behavior so that you can be an attentive, fun-loving, responsive partner.

2. Meet your own needs.

We all have needs. They are different from "wants" and "coulds" because a need <u>must</u> be met. It is not optional. If our needs are not met, our development slows down. If our needs aren't met, we try to meet them in dysfunctional ways, and we attract other needy people. Our needs run **us**. Our unsatisfied needs push us to compromise our standards, to be less than we would want to be ideally.

When we have our needs met, we have room for love and caring. We are self-confident and self-reliant. So get your needs met. Figure out what your primary needs are at this time. For instance, if you have a need for money, instead of marrying to get it, figure out how you will satisfy this need for yourself, either by making more or spending less. If you don't meet this need by yourself, it could drive you to be with someone that isn't perfect for you.

Another example would be feeling that you need a mother or father for your child. Again, admit to this need and find a way to satisfy it. Perhaps another family member or friend could fill this role. Or maybe playgroups or church groups could help provide parenting. By getting the need met, you don't have to choose someone out of a compulsion to have another parent for your child. You are then free to choose based on values and desires instead of needs.

Until you make peace with who you are,
You'll never be content with what you have.
Doris Mortman

3. Free yourself from dead-end relationships.

If you are involved with a **married person,** where does **that** take you? Even if they promise, "Someday I'll get a divorce," believe it when you see it.

Ask yourself–

- Why am I doing this?
- Am I holding out hope that they will eventually leave their spouse? [Realize that leaving the current spouse makes it easier to leave the next one.]
- Or, am I here because it is safe and I don't have to commit?

If you have been hanging on with a person that simply **won't commit** to you or take the relationship further to where you want it, you're still at ground zero. How are you going to achieve lift-off? Stop holding out hope and making excuses for this partner. It is time to say good-bye. People who are commitment-phobic will make you think that they are right there, but they never seem to take the step you would like. Ask yourself:

- Do I feel left out of any of their thoughts? If you notice that they consult you only after they make a decision, question that.
- Do they include me in all phases of their life? With family? And friends?

We'll talk more about the commitment-phobic partner in **Chapter 4**.

If you spend all your time with friends who are not potential partners, where is this going to lead? While fun and safe, these friends may be a dead-end when it comes to having a romantic relationship.

Why do we stay too long in dead-end relationships? We are **afraid**. We are afraid of the **void**, to be **alone** or to be **lonely**. It's a couples' society. We think it is better to have <u>someone</u> there than to be all alone—so we choose to compromise. We are afraid of the unknown. Maybe there is no one better. We don't trust that what might be out there could be better than what we have, even though what we have is not healthy nor good for us.

In a cartoon, a young woman describes her beau as the "been-trying-to-break-up-with-me-for-five-years-but afraid-to-go-ahead-with-it" type. Is this you? If so, what is it getting you?

We are afraid of **change**. We also fear **confrontation**. If we ask for what we want, we fear that we will be rejected, abandoned or left. It takes self-knowledge to know exactly what it is that we want for ourselves, and then it takes courage to stand up and ask for it.

We are afraid of **being the bad guy,** the one to actually leave the relationship, especially knowing that we are hurting someone else. We worry more about them than us. We sacrifice ourselves to avoid hurting them. When we do this, we are not taking care of us.

Are you in a relationship that is verbally, physically or emotionally **abusive?**

Each of these makes you feel small and disempowered. Someone who puts you down verbally, hits you or plays games with your mind is toxic. The sooner you leave, the faster you can heal yourself and go on to a healthy relationship.

You may feel **threatened** by your partner's violent behavior if you do leave, and so you stay. Many a case of domestic violence—and many a death—has been due to the fear of walking away from an abusive partner. If you try to leave and your partner threatens retaliation or suicide, you freeze in fear.

Sometimes you convince yourself that it's easier to just live with it. But if you were content to live with what you have, you wouldn't be reading this book, would you?

So get the courage, either by reminding yourself that beyond your closed door lies the freedom to find happiness, or by getting support from friends and counselors or, in the case of fear of violence, getting help through anger management and/or police authorities.

Remember that before you can pursue the path to your future, you have to close the door to your past.

4. Lead a full, balanced life.

To meet interesting people, it is easier if <u>you</u> are interesting. If you have a full, interesting life, you will always have something to share and a method to draw other interesting people to you.

Take a look at the "Wheel of Life" diagram to see just how in or out of balance your life is today. Disregard the relationship sector. We'll work on that together. Examine the other categories. What would it take to make each segment a 10? Then get to work on it. This is where a coach can assist you in sorting out exactly what you want in your life and how to get it. Ask yourself, "What are my passions? What do I just love to do?" Then do them **now** and get your own life. Do not wait for a mate to bring you happiness.

> *A career is wonderful, but you can't*
> *curl up with a career on a cold night.*
> *Marilyn Monroe*

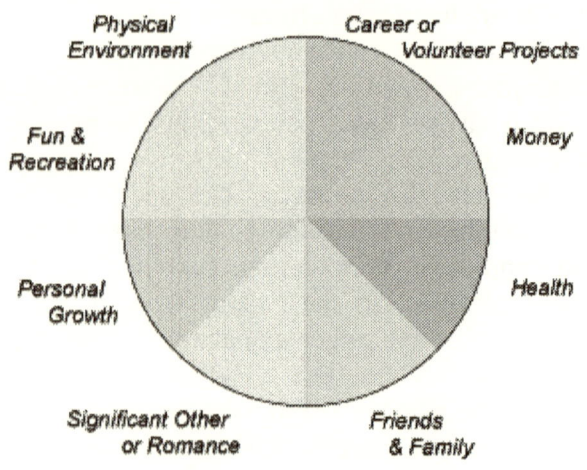

Wheel of Life

Physical Environment — Career or Volunteer Projects — Money — Health — Friends & Family — Significant Other or Romance — Personal Growth — Fun & Recreation

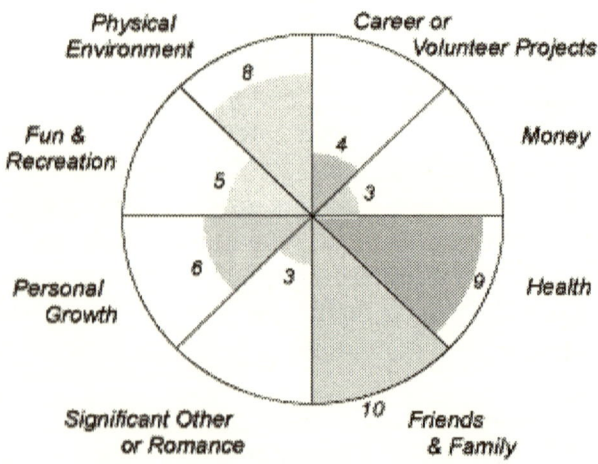

Example

5. Possess a positive attitude.

Research shows that we are attracted to people who are attracted to us. It's called the Law of Reciprocity. Internet dating research also concludes that one attribute that men are really attracted to in women is confidence.

When we are in a good mood, we feel happy, satisfied, excited, and curious. We show greater interest in others, and we are friendlier.

Smile, make eye contact and say hello to people. This might be difficult if you are not used to doing it. So fake it at first if you have to and test the results. If you need help being positive, listen to good music, watch an uplifting movie, or listen to a funny tape.

Look at the glass half-full. And count your blessings. Literally. Each day list five good things in your life.

6. Be kind

Women talk of men who are cruel to them because they're not beautiful enough, and men complain about women who are dismissive because they don't make enough money. According to recent studies on authentic happiness by Martin Seligman, wealth, looks, education, status, youth and health won't make you any happier than you usually are. But being in a group of supportive friends and being in a good marriage will.

One woman—not so attractive—told me how she met and married her very attractive husband. When he came to the door on an arranged date, she invited him in for a drink, and she actually had food in her refrigerator and asked if he'd like something to eat. As a matter of fact, he would, and she prepared him a little snack. It wasn't just "Where are you taking me?" She was kind and cared about his welfare.

7. Present an attractive appearance.

Appearance isn't <u>everything</u>, but let's face it, it's not <u>nothing</u> either.

Research suggests that men still notice beauty first and then character. Women notice character and then attractiveness. Appearance includes clothes, cleanliness, neatness, style and weight.

- Do you practice good grooming?
- Does your makeup enhance your looks?
- Are your clothes flattering, right for you and conveying the image you want to have?
- Do you dress authentically, expressing who you are?

Would **you** be attracted to **you**? People usually fall in love with others of similar attractiveness. And this is a good thing. To fall in love with someone who is much more attractive would probably just make you jealous and suspicious.

I've always considered myself fairly attractive except when I was engaged to a man who was downright gorgeous. Living in New York City at the time, we couldn't walk down a street without his turning heads. I started doubting my own attractiveness, my ability to keep him interested, and his faithfulness.

If you want to up the attractiveness quotient of the people you attract, you're going to have to up your own first. I believe this is the reason for the success of such shows as *Queer Eye for the Straight Guy and Date Patrol*. So watch these shows. Get help. Take action now rather than fooling yourself that you can sneak by somehow. You can't.

And while we're on the subject of appearance, I'd like to quote the three men from *Marry Me* who say to women,

"Your chest may be something that initially attracts a man to you, but in terms of getting a man to commit to a long-term relationship, rest assured that breast size has nothing to do with it. I laugh at those explosive breasts some women have implanted. Women who choose such a front are not for the professional man. I don't want to be seen or associated with a grotesque, out of proportion embarrassment."

Appearance Assessment

What are the one or two things that you could undertake immediately that would improve your appearance?

I could: (for example, I could shave my beard, style my hair, lose 10 pounds)

1.

2.

**Therefore, as part of my Partner Project
I will:** (for example, I will call Rachel for a hair appointment, go through my closet and throw out apparel that no longer fits or flatters me)

1.

2.

Appearance Assessment (continued)

Or, I have decided that I will not make these changes and here is why:

1.

2.

By **not** making these changes as part of my project, I acknowledge that I will not be the person I could become. I am content to accept that these inactions may lessen my ability to find the perfect partner.

Signature_____ Date   /

If you are not certain about your appearance and image and you want to explore these, there are image consultants who help people do just that. Or sometimes an honest friend or a younger sister will do the job.

Stage 3 of the Partnership Project: Setting your Guidelines

The final step in getting ready to date is to know who you are. This means what you want, what you don't want, what you demand. Better to know your desires and requirements **before** you start out so you don't get confused or in trouble down the road.

1. Discover your Values.

Values, in coaching, describe what you are naturally inclined, drawn or eager to do, without effort or prompting. They are what are important for you to lead a rewarding, successful life. If you orient your life around your values, you will lead a fulfilling life. Fulfillment is that inner feeling beyond happiness or satisfaction-it's the feel of being totally you and having worth. It's who you "be."

Below is a list of questions that will help you identify your values. There are no good or bad values, just the ones which are important to you and the ones with which you want to pilot your life.

Take out a pad of paper and answer the following:
1. What do you love to do professionally and/or personally?
2. What are the most significant or meaningful personal and/or professional accomplishments in your life?
3. What are you naturally to other people personally and/or professionally? Are you a teacher? Motivator? Nurturer? Leader? Adventurer? Follower? Other?
4. What did you love to do as a kid or young adult that you have gotten away from now?
5. What past experience was the most painful for you?
6. What past experience brought you the most joy?
7. What pain do you not want yourself or others ever to feel?
8. What joy do you not want yourself or others to be without?
9. When do you feel so immersed in something that you forget that the rest of the world exists?
10. If you could do anything in the world that you wanted to, what would it be?
11. What would you most like the people at your funeral to say about you, specifically?
12. Who in history do you admire most, and why?

13. What is the inkling you have of your purpose or vision?
14. If it weren't important to have a life purpose, what would you most like to do in the next decade?
15. What are the qualities you need to express in yourself or your life to feel happy?

Having gone through this assessment, what then are your main values in life?

They could be:

Accomplishment/results, adventure/excitement, achievement, aesthetics/beauty, authenticity, autonomy, clarity, commitment, community, connecting/bonding, creativity, education/knowledge, equality, ethics, excellence/mastery, freedom, humor, inspiration, integrity/honesty, intimacy, joy, justice, leadership, learning, love, loyalty, mental health, originality, partnership, peace, personal growth, physical health, power, privacy/solitude, productivity, relationships, respect, risk, romance, safety, security, spirituality, success, teaching, tradition, trust, vitality/zest or any number of others.

Circle the top 10 values associated with your answers. After you've circled them, list the top five. The most precious one of these is your deepest value. (Warning: This is not an easy exercise.)

My top five values are:
1.

2.

3.

4.

5.

2. Decide what you require in a perfect significant other.

Knowing what your values are, what are the most important characteristics in a partner for you? What do you want in an ideal relationship? Describe your ideal partner below. (Hint: Couples who have similar values are best able to relate to one another's dreams and goals.)

Age
Religion
Ethnic background or race
Financial worth
Marital history
Children
Education
Career
Attitude
Sensitivity
Curiosity level
Energy level
Others

Here's a word of advice from Marianne Williamson. "Make your list of what you want in a relationship. Would he date you? You have to become the person you want to attract."

Revisit here what you decided you needed to change in your <u>own</u> life, to ensure you're worthy to be the partner of the person you want.

Remember that the more you limit your options, the narrower will be the field. On the other hand, if you feel strongly about the issue, put it down so as not to be playing in the wrong ballpark. In fact, some researchers find that the irritating habits that make you crazy may be a stronger factor in mate selection than the traits that you are drawn to. So write down any trait that's an automatic deal-breaker. Smoking, drugs, tattoos, degree of hirsuteness, children? (Internet-dating research shows the biggest "can't-stands" are liars and people who can't control their anger.)

We most often pick partners who are similar to us in family background, religion, psychological hang-ups, values, psychological maturity and tendency to addiction. It's always interesting, when working with couples where one partner seems so much more together than the other, to wait and see the hang-ups appear in the seemingly stable person. They always do. Again, water seeks its own level.

Write a profile of your ideal mate:

Now that you know what you want in a partner, let's look at how you want the **relationship** to be.

3. Defining your boundaries.

A boundary is an imaginary line of protection that you draw around yourself. It protects you from the unhealthy or damaging behavior of others. Boundaries are about what others cannot do **to** you or **around** you, what you will not **tolerate**. You cannot get what you want without boundaries.

Boundaries help you trust yourself and raise your self-esteem because you won't allow bad things to happen to you. Do you have your boundaries written down? Do you know what they are? A coach can help you with setting boundaries if you need help defining them. Or you can ask yourself the questions:

- What behavior will I not tolerate?
- What can't people do around me or to me?
- What treatment will I not excuse or condone?

An example of setting a boundary would be to promise yourself, "I will not tolerate someone who drinks so much that I am uncomfortable being around them." Or "I will accept that my partner has two children, but I will <u>not</u> tolerate those children being disrespectful."

A very beautiful client, an Audrey Hepburn look-alike, had reached the point where she was refusing to date. Why? Her dates did not show her any respect; they immediately pushed to have sex with her. She was upset and didn't know what to do.

Fulfillment is essentially a relationship between yourself
and your personal values and conscience.
John F. Reynolds III

But the answer was simple. She didn't have to stop dating. She only needed to set her boundaries. By simply being able to state what wasn't acceptable and what she wouldn't allow, she could happily resume dating. (See more on sexual boundaries in Chapter Two.)

This is where you profit from all the bad experiences that you've had before. This is where you list all the things you promised yourself that you would never tolerate again. Here is where you can protect yourself from repeating the same mistakes over again. Be firm in your boundaries and make them two to three times bigger than you think they should be.

Set your boundaries

State what you will never tolerate from a partner.
1. Too much alcohol?
2. Drug use?
3. Someone who forces physical intimacy on you?
4. A self-centered, narcissistic person?
5. Being left alone at functions so you feel alone and abandoned?
6. For the woman, having to pay the bill?
7. Foul language?
8. What else?

If you are creating your boundaries for the first time, educate others about them gently. Make sure that you are heard when doing so. Closely related to boundaries are

4. Elevating your standards.

Personal standards set the behavior and actions to which you are willing to hold <u>yourself</u> accountable. Maybe some of your standards have been too low in the past. This leads to problems, which then may lead to lack of self-esteem.

By setting behavioral standards, "stuff" that you don't want stops coming into your life. You tolerate less naturally, and you develop higher integrity and self-esteem. You also have less for which to be embarrassed or ashamed.

Clean up your life before you meet someone new. Once you live with higher standards, you won't want to return to that level of weakness, being out of control, or waking up and panicking, "Oh my gosh, what did I do"?

In their book, *Marry Me*, the three authors talk about "good for now girls" and "marrying material." Their Ugly Truth #4 states "if you want a man to marry you, you'd better leave your baggage at home in the closet. When he is with his girlfriend, he wants to relax, have fun, make love, and enjoy her company. He does not want to play the role of shrink. If a woman has a ton of problems—and can never seem to deal with them herself—then a man will be turned off."

If you have broken up with a partner, do not allow them to remain your friend. Seeing each other or chatting on the phone, unless it is strictly business, won't work.

And especially don't do booty calls, sex on a "just friends" level with an old partner. This keeps you entangled and keeps you from being out looking for the

All discarded lovers should be given a
second chance, but with somebody else.
Mae West

<u>right</u> person. Really, **really** don't do them with an ex spouse if you have children. The kids will fantasize that Mom and Dad might get back together, which will be heart-breaking when it doesn't happen.

If you just **have** to have sex, masturbate. Or try sublimation.

There are reasons that you broke up. They're still there. Do you want to get sucked back into your old behaviors? You need a clean break, which is sometimes difficult.

But by setting your boundaries and raising your standards, you will protect yourself from situations that devastated you in the past. This takes strength, courage, and a belief in yourself that you are better off alone than with the wrong partner.

So state here, and keep stating it:

I am better off alone than with the wrong partner.

Now that you have the right mental attitude, full of confidence and hope; the right standards and boundaries in place to protect you; the right outward appearance; and the past behind you, not intruding in your present or future plans, it's time to start . . .

When we can make decisions from an open heart, then we are able to create a better life.
John Gray

 **Chapter Two – Dating**

The Dating phase starts when you begin to take action on your Partnership Project and ends at commitment.

I could spend time here commiserating about how tough the dating scene is, how there just aren't eligible singles out there, that it's like a meat market, yada yada yada. But why bother? Just accept that the road to commitment starts with tiny steps called "Dates," and there are no detours.

Now that you've got your determination back, what do you do?

1. Filling the Pipeline.

Dating is a numbers game, just as Sales is in business. When you are marketing a product or service, you must get out there and talk to many people in order to sell it to a few. You don't wait for clients to come to you!

Or, when job hunting, you eventually have to go for the personal interview, don't you? Dates? Same thing. You have to bite the bullet, get out and schmooze, and sell yourself!

"Oh no, oh no, I could never do that," I hear you saying. "I'm too shy, I'm too awkward, and I never know what to say." Calma. Calma. Take a deep breath.

You do it every day you know. You probably do it in business. There's probably something that you sell. Whether it's your product, your expertise, or your thinking capacity, you are selling yourself.

You want dating to be about having options. You are going to date many different people—people you never dreamed you'd date—to be able to have many choices.

In Sales, they refer to finding as many prospective clients as possible as "Filling the Pipeline." The better and bigger the list of prospects you can potentially sell to, the larger the number of prospective deals in the pipeline, and the better your chances of making the deal.

Likewise, to meet your perfect partner, you're going to have to fill the pipeline. That means meeting them, going out with them and getting to know them. And **then** you can decide whether they're a keeper or not. The last part we'll get into later, in the Rating chapter. Right now, however, you need to be ready, willing and eager to meet new people.

If you can't do this, you're back where you began, waiting, hoping that the right person is going to magically appear before you and sweep you off your feet. Highly Unlikely!!

So here is the commitment you need to make **right now.**

I am ready, willing and able to move my project to the dating level. I am willing to look for candidates that I might want to date.

Signature _____ Date   /   /

> Or
>
> I am **not** willing to take the risk of finding possible dates. I am content to do **nothing** and wait for the right person to appear. I realize that in doing this, my chances of meeting a suitable partner have diminished to almost zero. I am willing to accept this future.
>
> Signature_____Date   /   /

2. Looking in the right places.

Research by psychosociologist Ayala Pines indicates that the closer you are to a person, the more apt you are to fall in love. It's the result of repeated exposure. Only 11% of people fall in love at first sight, so for the rest it's a matter of seeing the person over and over. We fall in love with people that we work with, are on teams with, and who live in the neighborhood.

In an experiment, Pines used four very attractive women as supposed participants in a particular class. One went to zero classes; one, to one class; one, to ten; and one, to 15. Afterward Pines showed their pictures to their classmates. The one who attended the most was liked the most. The one who didn't attend at all was liked the least. The more the woman attended, the more she was perceived to be attractive, intelligent, interesting and similar to the rest of the class.

So maybe *Melrose Place* is right. Live somewhere where the kind of people you are attracted to are in your close physical environment.

General locale

Is your area loaded with eligible dates? Or do you live in a village of Trappist monks? As long as you're going fishing, you might as well pick a pond that's loaded with fish. A stocked stream makes the fishing more fun and the outcome infinitely better.

Here's a list of cities where there are plenty of singles, defined as residents aged 25 to 34.

City	#	Pct. of total population
Atlanta	464,015	15%
Austin	154,259	17%
Boston	395,867	15%
Chicago	808,470	13%
Cincinnati	139,537	12%
Louisville	86,435	11%
Memphis	97,015	12%
Milwaukee	133,185	12%
Pittsburgh	185,077	10%
Richmond, Va.	90,203	12%
San Francisco	247,558	18%
Seattle	284,320	15%
Tampa/St Pete's	176,012	9%
Washington D.C.	542,418	15%

Many of the cities listed are deliberately trying to build communities to attract young people, so check them out. *Money* magazine has a guide to help you find the perfect place to live. Do some research at www. money.com.

I personally have also heard good things about
- Alaska—hey, I know, not for everyone, but if you're an adventuresome, outdoor type, it could work.

- Marina del Rey—It's the divorce capital of California. Twenty-one percent of residents there are divorced, as opposed to 10% in the rest of the state.
- Texas—Houston and Dallas have lots of available men, and they're all gentlemen.
- San Francisco—The word on the street is that all the men in San Francisco are gay. Not so! Lots of good fishing here.

For clients who love where they're living and don't want to move, I tell them to move anyway. If possible, for six months. Don't sell your house. Don't give up the job of a lifetime. But if your number one priority is finding a mate, move! Then marry the partner and bring them back to the place you love.

If you're where they're **not**, consider moving. Seriously! If you want to find wild animals, you go to Africa. If you want to hunt elk, you go to Montana. And if you want to catch a marlin, go to Hawaii. There are too many fish in the sea to keep casting into a dried-up hole.

Specific locale

Go to places alone. When you are with a group of friends, you tend to stick together and not put yourself forward. Go to parties, movies, lectures, museums, and parks by yourself. If you feel bold, you might even draw subtle attention to yourself with a cute dog or by roller-blading in a sports-bra or both. (You're reminding me that you're a male? Just think of how much attention you'd get. Depending on personal preference.)

In a local newspaper the readers' top choices for places to meet people were church and Adult Education classes.

Other places to be:

1. Volunteer at your favorite charity or on a political campaign. It helps if you're genuinely interested in the cause. When you exude enthusiasm, others will be drawn to you.

2. Regularly frequent coffee houses and have breakfast out at the same place. You need a place like *Cheers* where everybody knows your name.

3. Join or start a Single's Dinner Club. Take turns being the host. Have the dinner once a week or once a month. Have people invite new friends all the time. It can be as easy as a potluck.

4. Begin a co-ed evening book club

5. Go on blind dates. Carefully. Forty-five percent of singles have never tried one, and 21% say they'd rather have a root canal. But if we meet most people through family and friends, don't these point to blind dates? So consider trying it.

Remember that there's a difference between a blind date arranged for a woman by a guy and by another woman. A guy arranges a blind date for his buddy because the friend needs some sex. Period. Women arrange a date for a friend with some consideration of what the people are like.

Men like blind dates because they know the woman is willing and able to date. She won't blow him off, as she might if he met her somewhere and called. The woman will be receptive to his initial attempts to get together.

Blind dates are an excellent alternative to the bar scene where you meet no one. Each blind date brings a possibility to fall in love. On blind dates, looks are extremely important. A man can only see the cover. He wants a woman to look nice without overdoing the makeup, be well groomed, and be dressed nicely without being a fashion victim.

6. Blind-date swap. If you've gone out with someone that's a great person but not your type, find someone else who blind dates and swap with them.

7. Have Sunday brunch at a fun restaurant with friends. Each friend brings one to five other single friends each week.

8. Regularly shop at the same bookstore.

9. Participate in team sports such as softball, volleyball, tennis or soccer. Play golf by yourself and ask to be teamed in a foursome.

According to Nita Tucker, author of *How Not to Stay Single*, ten good places for men to meet women are:

> Getting involved in the Arts
> Cooking classes
> Arts and crafts classes
> Fashion shows
> Horse shows
> Aerobic classes
> Yoga classes
> Cosmetic counters
> Dance classes
> Garden clubs and tours.

And ten good places for women to meet men are:

> Golf courses or driving ranges

> Computer stores
> Hardware stores
> Car auctions or rallies
> Auto-supply stores
> Sporting events
> Fly-fishing classes
> Boat shows
> Skeet-shooting classes and
> Political events

Still other places to meet people are:
1. A gym
2. River rafting
3. A bicycling group
4. A hiking group
5. A martial art class such as judo, Aikido or karate
6. A reunion
7. Courses that really interest you such as writing, painting, computers or wine selection
8. A sports' bar during football season

The Arousal Concept.

Ayala Pines finds that a person who is in the high physiological arousal state that accompanies strong emotion is ripe to fall in love. Starting a new job, a change in residence, a painful loss, and/or a threat of death can all put someone in a hyper-aroused state that makes them more open to love.

She cites the Capilano River study. In this study, there are two bridges crossing the river. One is a rope bridge that tends to tilt, sway and wobble. It has very low handrails making it hard to hold on. And it has a 230-foot drop to rocks below. The other bridge, the control bridge, is sturdy, 10 feet above the water, has high handrails and doesn't tilt. Which one would you rather use?

The men were divided into two groups. Each man, after he crossed the bridge, was given a Thematic Apperception Test card picturing a woman, clothed, holding her head, by a door. Each man was also told that he could call the very attractive interviewer if he had questions. The men who crossed the rickety bridge wrote stories with many more sexual and romantic themes. And eight times more of them called the interviewer!

This seems somewhat similar to the Stockholm Syndrome where women who are held captive over time fall in love with the man who holds them in captivity.

Another example Pines gives is Folk-dancing love. This occurs with people who are folk-dancing addicts. Combining the physical arousal from the dancing and the emotional arousal inspired by the tunes or the words of the song increases the dancer's natural attraction to the partner. They get excited and sexually turned on and think they are madly in love rather than just aroused by the Virginia reel.

So consider activities with high physical and emotional arousal possibilities: hiking, aerobics, jogging, trips abroad, action movies, exciting concerts and spiritual journeys. Even external obstacles, like distance, disapproving parents or jail can enhance attraction.

Getting them to come to you.

If you don't have the time, the stamina or the personality to actively look for partners, here are some armchair ideas.

An ad
A dating service
The Internet

An ad.

Place an ad in your local newspaper. Carefully. In writing the ad, show your sense of humor. Remember you are selling yourself, and not too many people are attracted to Cruella de Ville. Be accurate; if you are tall, say so in a clever way.

Don't include your telephone number; use a post office box. When you receive a response, be discriminating. Listen to your intuition.

In **answering** ads, be wary. Assume that people embellish. Take all claims lightly and decipher for yourself.

The Advice Ladies, Amy Alkon, Caroline Johnson, and MarloI Minnick, three New York City women who wrote *Free Advice*, decipher the Personals for their readers:

- "Strong, virile and handsome" means hairy back
- "Rubenesque" means full-figured, cuddly, shapely – fat
- "All calls answered" means desperate
- "Honest" means a whining bore
- "Secure with myself" means has done EST and The Forum
- "Cute and chunky guy" means physique resembles cantaloupe placed on top of the refrigerator
- "Sculptor, artist, musician, Bohemian, aspiring writer" means destitute, you pay

If you find someone that sounds genuine and interesting, meet this person for the first time in a public place, **never in your home**, never at a regular watering hole. You don't know what's really behind the virtuous hero in the ad.

A dating service.

Valenti International charges $10,000. Very expensive and upper crust. Others are less. Checkmates, in San Francisco, bills itself as a dating service for upscale professionals. A similar one is It's Just Lunch. Founded in 1991, it now has 50 offices and more than 20,000 clients. It claims that so far roughly 10,000 marriages have resulted.

If you don't want to begin with a one-on-one encounter, there's also Table for Six, a dating service that puts together dinners for six people of similar background.

If you're really in a hurry, there's Speed dating. It involves a large number of people at a big party, with a set rotation schedule. A couple spends eight minutes "dating" and then the bell rings. They move on to the next person. The evening is the equivalent of eight 8-minute dates, and it costs about $4 a chat.

Sound fun? It's kind of like a round-robin tennis tournament, with flirtatious interrogation between strangers. There's also **8minuteDating** in Manhattan and Boston**; Fast Dater** in the Midwest - $35 for 40 three-minute dates; and **HurryDate** in Atlanta.

Many of these agencies can sort by age, sexual preference, race, religion or interest. Check first to see how much they charge and what they promise in return. Remember that their potential partners are only going to be as good as the people who contact them.

Love doesn't drop on you unexpectedly; you have to give off signals, sort of like an amateur radio operator.
Helen Gurley Brown

The Internet.

There are 40 million singles in America right now, and half of them visited an online dating site last month. Barbara Dafoe Whitehead, co-director of the National Marriage Project at Rutgers University, says that " this is as important [a change] as the automobile was in the 1920's and birth control in the 1960's."

Thank heavens for the high-tech age. Some of the best services, match.com and Love.com, work this way:

For $25 or so per month you can search their files. Specify what age range you would like and a few other characteristics. You can give a specific geographic location to within a five-mile radius.

You can receive up to 5-6 pages of potential dates, for a total of 50 – 60 people. For each person they include, they report what percentage match this person is with your qualifications.

The benefits of on-line dating services are that you can pre-screen who you'll go out with, which saves a lot of time and is a fast way to vet potential dates. And, while many of us have trouble dating because of some quirky characteristic, with large numbers of people, many may find this characteristic endearing.

Busy professionals like to find dates online. They can meet people and move the relationship along more quickly. It saves them time, they can do the research from their office, and it is like going on a blind date that they've set up for themselves.

Older singles like it also. More than 20% of the searchers are 50 or older.

It exposes you to thousands of potential dates—more than you'd ever meet in a year . . . or ten.

And several of the sites have become more sophisticated. They use psychological testing now. Match.com uses software to study personality traits and then report back to users on what percentage of the dating population would be attracted to their personality characteristics. Eharmony.com has a 480-question assessment of personality traits and "Basic subconscious wants." They also find what the client "Can't Stand."

I have heard more success stories from online dating than anywhere else so I push people to try it.

The drawbacks are that

- The candidates presented are only as good as the people who use the service.
- Reportedly, for one good potential partner there are 7-8 bad ones.
- Sometimes it takes a long time between chats.
- Women don't trust men online and won't give out information. The man may start feeling like a molester.
- There is too much over-analysis.

But I insist that my clients try it. I ask them to browse first. At each site they do a search, based on a couple of factors like age or location or education. Does the site seem to fit? Does it make them feel old, dowdy, young, staid?

Then they choose two, one a general site and one a specialty site, and post their profile on them.

General sites beside Match, Love and eHarmony are

- American Singles.com
- Date.com
- Yahoo. personal. com

Specific sites are:

- Christiandates.com, $29/month.

- JDate.com., a Jewish singles site with over 500,000 members. If your mother told you to marry a nice Jewish boy, this is your place.
- Rightstuffdating.com, for graduates from the top schools in *U.S. News* ratings, who want to date other Ivy Leaguers, $70 for six months.
- SeniorFriendFinder.com, 750,000 members, $22 for 3 months.
- ThirdAgeConnections.com for people in their 40s, 50s, and 60s. 1.5 million members, $20/month.

The one I recommend to most people is Eharmony. It takes time to fill out the initial assessment. Hours, maybe. But I like it because it was developed by Neil Clark Warren, who in his book, *Date…or Soul Mate?,* states that blind dating is a waste of time and that to find your soul mate you need to have essential qualities in common. This sounds a lot like the Values clarification and Partner Profile, yes?

I hope you see by the numbers that while you're procrastinating, millions of other people are doing it. With Success! Internet dating is mainstream now. So do it!

When Posting your Profile.

- Have an intriguing Header, one that shows you at your best as a partner.
- Show your personality…cleverly. Don't be single, over 45, widower. Be a "reformed pragmatist."
- Be truthful. People really can pick out the dishonest profiles after they've searched for a while. Don't be God's gift to women or Ben Affleck's next honey. Be upbeat and honest.

- Specify what you want in a positive way, i.e., "Looking for the mother for my child" rather than "Fat women need not apply."
- Update your profile every few days. On most sites, the new and updated profiles appear at the top.
- Do a photo. In fact, do a mini-album. Show yourself doing the things that you love. If you don't have a digital camera, you'll probably have to have the photo shop put the pictures in jpg form for you on a CD.
- Make sure the photos are current and you look attractive and something like your real self. Dotcom daters don't want a surprise. So, truth in advertising, please.
- When you respond, be complimentary and curious. Remember **reciprocity**? We are attracted to people who are attracted to us.

Talking via the Internet.

Internet dating sites now have audio features, which means you can talk live to the person, without divulging your phone number. Some have Instant Messaging. Others, like excite.com and altavista.com have chat rooms. There are ones for lawyers, doctors, computer programmers, real estate agents, accountants, executives and many others. Find the specific chat room you want, such as "married with children" or "in my thirties" and click in. Or name your own chat room, using an alias of course.

Most chat rooms are free; some have monthly dues.

Don't let the audio, instant messaging or e-mail exchange go on too long. After five talks, if you like the person, set an in-person date, taking safety precautions. Find out if they're for you sooner rather than later. If your photo isn't posted, consider sending a picture early into the e-mailing. It shows good faith and can save time if the other really isn't interested.

Now that you've considered the possibilities, what are you going to do? This week? Daily?

Create your own weekly action plan on how you will fill your pipeline. Use the following form on a weekly basis. I suggest that you **copy it before filling it in.**

Love is anticipation and memory, uncertainty and longing. It's unreasonable, of course. Nothing begins with so much excitement and hope and pleasure as love, except maybe writing a story. And like a story, love must be troubled to be interesting. We crave love, can't live without its intimacy though it pains us. Every person in therapy has a love disorder: never felt love, can't find love, trapped by love, unraveled by love, thinks love is lust or love is loss, fears love, loves too much, uses love for profit, jealous in love, lost in love, love affairs, unrequited love, love sick, doesn't love Mom, won't love Dad, can't love the kids, can't love the self, hopeless love, self-absorbed love, love as a crutch, love as a love lost, secret love, love on the run, love that hates truncheon, love in ruins, crazy love, love that eats the heart, careless love, drowning in love, love that dares not speak its name, blind love, consuming love, obsessive love, conditional love, dangerous love, first love, last love, fickle love, love and marriage, dutiful love, borrowed love, thief of love, love in embers, love in vain, love in shackles, love maligned, love that warps the mind a little.

John Dufresne, Love Warps the Mind a Little.

My Action Plan for Finding the Perfect Partner

I accept that finding the ideal partner will take on "Partner-Project" status for me.

_____

      Signature

This week of _____ I will:

Getting Ready: (Choose 3)

☐   Free myself by disentangling from current relationships that aren't working.

☐   Free myself by getting closure on past relationships.

☐   Analyze what I did wrong in the past in order to correct it.

☐   Build Attractiveness by listing 10 things I love about my body.

☐   Build Attractiveness by listing 10 characteristics I love about my self.

☐   Re-evaluate my wardrobe and my appearance.

☐   Improve my current life situation.

☐   Re-examine my boundaries and standards.

☐   Take action to deal with my fear(s).

☐   Make my life full and abundant.

☐   List five blessings.

Making it Happen: (Choose 3 - 5)

☐   Call five friends to ask for introductions to potential dates.

☐   Scout out a comfortable breakfast, lunch or coffee spot where I can meet potential dates and go 3 – 5 times per week.

☐   Place an ad.

☐   Answer an ad.

☐   Go to a specific place to meet partners.

☐   Smile at 50 people.

☐   Plan a Singles's Dinner Club.

☐   Arrange a blind date.

☐   Try blind-date swapping.

☐   Register with a dating service.

☐   Register with an online dating service.

☐   Join a sports' team

☐   Others

_____

_____

_____

The Reward (Choose 1)

☐ Do something that is attuned to my Values.

☐ Visualize success daily.

☐ Schedule a day of fun.

☐ Talk to a friend who can give me support.

☐ Acknowledge myself for taking the initiative.

☐ Write in my B-M-W (Bitch – Moan – Whine) journal about rejection

---

I know that by following my Action Plan, I will improve my chances of finding the Perfect Partner. Therefore, I will carry out the action plan <u>and</u> if I do what I have committed to do, for the sake of my own happiness, I will reward myself by:

Signature_____

I know that if I don't follow through with my Action Plan, if I allow shyness, tiredness, hopelessness, or _____ (Honestly fill in your reason to not do something) to keep me from following through, I will be no farther ahead toward finding the Perfect Partner than when I began. I am willing to be in limbo, waiting for romance to find <u>me</u>.
Signature_____

After a few weeks, if you've been diligently, patiently, and without expectations, taking the steps to fill your pipeline, you now have candidates to actually date. If you do <u>not</u>, re-examine what you are doing, especially whether the pond is full of live fish or is dried up.

My pipeline is not filling up. I think the reasons could be

1. I am not following my Action Plan. I will start again on _____.

2. Potential dates are not at the places I am going. I need to devise a new Action Plan.

3. I am in the wrong general locale. I need to change my residence.

4. I am still in the Pre-dating Stage. I have not made the right mental or physical changes to be available and attractive.

5. I am still involved with someone else.

I will make the following corrections to my plan:

1.

2.

3.

If you are on course, the next step in your project is...

The First Date and Beyond

This includes:
1. Meeting people
2. Making the date
3. Deciding where to go
4. What to talk about
5. What not to talk about
6. What not to do
7. Touching

But first, most importantly, it includes an understanding of:

The Three-Date Rule

Here's the deal. I want you to commit that anyone you go out with once, you'll consent to go out with three times. Anyone. Even if the first date is a disaster. **Especially** if the first date is a disaster. Here's why.

1. Sometimes you can't judge a book by its cover, and the beauty that's within isn't revealed immediately. You have to get to know a person slowly over a period of time to make an intelligent decision and choice about them.
2. Depending on your sexual persuasion, everyone wants to be with Tom Cruise, Pierce Brosnan, Halle Berry, Faith Hill. Why do you want them? "Ooh, imagine the chemistry."

That's right. Everyone is looking for **chemistry**.

But remember when I asked you to define your Values and then asked you to describe your ideal partner? Probably very little of what you came up with had to do with that pzzzt!! kind of chemistry.

3. More scientifically, a survey of over 2000 happily married couples, in committed long-term relationships, when asked if they had any chemistry when they first met, 90 percent, yes, **90% said no**!

We're attracted to what we know. Much as we hate to admit it, there's a lot of Mom-Dad stuff going on with chemistry. According to Jeffrey Young in his book, *Re-Inventing Your Life*, many people develop "Lifetraps" from the way they were treated in their childhood. These Lifetraps may lead us, almost automatically, to a certain type of mate, one with whom we feel familiar, one with whom we may have **chemistry**.

So you should be wary of chemistry. Maybe it has gotten you into trouble in the past and is the reason you seem to attract the same, **wrong** mate all the time. I'll talk more about Lifetraps in Chapter 3. But whether you love him or hate her, the Three-Date Rule rules! Now let's discuss what to do when you have that . . .

*There are three possible parts to a date, of which at least two must be offered: entertainment, food, and affection. It is customary to begin a series of dates with a great deal of entertainment, a moderate amount of food, and the merest suggestion of affection. As the amount of affection increases, the entertainment can be reduced proportionately. When the affection **is** the entertainment, we not longer call it dating. Under no circumstances can food be omitted.*
Miss Manner's Guide to
Excruciatingly Correct Behavior

First Date.

1. Meeting people.

You want to make a good first impression. But how? Nicholas Boothman, in an article in *Bottom Line* titled "How to Make People Like You in 90 Seconds or Less," offers the following advice.

Smile. Smiles work wonders. Practice smiling till you can do it without looking strangled.

Notice eye color. This means you'll look in people's eyes. Don't stare, just notice. Poor eye contact suggests you have something to hide.

Use "open" body language. Keep your arms uncrossed and hands unclenched. Stand so you're square to the other person.

Mirror the other person's gestures and body language. If they laugh a lot, you laugh a lot; if they gesture wildly, you gesture wildly. After mirroring them for a while, change your movements and see if they'll go with you. If they do, they feel in sync. If they don't, continue matching them and then try again.

Ask open-ended questions. That means they can't be answered by a simple yes or no. Who, what, where, why, how, and when are the right words to start. If you're really shy, practice this with a friend. I had a client who needed two weeks of coaching to go directly to a "W" question and then be able to segue off the answer to another question. But once he got it, he felt comfortable talking to anyone because he knew he wouldn't get stranded conversationally and look like an idiot.

Relax. Boothman says that a Princeton University study found that trying too hard to be liked is a big turnoff. So do active relaxing. Take deep breaths. Imagine you're Sean Connery or Catherine Zeta Jones. Know that you have the right conversational skills to get you through.

2. Making the Date.

Warning, Warning. Ladies, think twice before asking the guys out. Why? There is still a courting etiquette in our society that dictates that men ask a woman out first. (I know it doesn't fit with being politically correct today, but sometimes "old fashioned" works the best.) Being the invitee tends to make some men nervous. On one hand they're flattered; on the other hand, they feel trapped and go to the place of "How do I get out of this and not hurt her feelings?"

There are other men who are delighted, honored and relieved to be asked out. It doesn't bother them a bit. In fact, two of my daughters met their significant others this way.

If you don't know which way he might go, here's what you can do. If a man you want to date does not ask you out, let him know that you would like him to. You may say, "I've really enjoyed talking with you. I'd love it if you would ask me out sometime." I have polled my classes and the women are relieved to hear that the guys would like this hint! Men tend to be risk averse. Many have a huge fear of rejection, so sometimes women need to encourage them.

Guys, actually ask the person out. Don't be vague. If you start by going out on a "kinda" date, you'll end up in a "kinda" relationship with someone who sees you as a "kinda" pal, with whom you'll have some friendly but not really romantic sex. When you are asking a woman out, please don't say, "Would you like to go out sometime?" Be specific. "Would you like to go see 'Bambi' with me on Wednesday night?" And ask one week in advance if possible. Never call for same-day dates unless you are well into the relationship and/or you've just been given a ticket for that evening. Otherwise, it's an insult to the woman.

If you are calling to make a first date, you don't have to give your life history over the phone. You just have to make a date. You can do the life history later.

If you do not know a person very well yet, keep your cool. Ladies, do not call him unless you are at least three dates into the relationship and know that he really likes you. It feels to guys that you are too aggressive and needy. They really do like to be the pursuer. If you want to see this super guy again, and he told you he would call you and he hasn't, even if your hand automatically goes toward that phone to call him, **don't**. Refrain. Short-term gratification makes for long-term regret. Chasing after a guy is a definite turn-off for him. If you've ever regretted making one too many phone calls to a man, then stop those dialing fingers.

3. Where to go for your first date(s.)

A. Restaurants

> Stay away from loud and noisy places where you can't hear each other.

B. Museums

> Wander through the halls and chat about what you like and don't like. This kind of date is relaxed, easy, inexpensive and a great way to get to know what appeals to the other person.

C. Amusement parks, fairs, festivals

> These are always fun and carefree.

D. Outdoor activities

    Sporting events, concerts, picnics, walks in the park can be very special.

E. Places of common interest

    Make sure you have the ability to talk and get to know each other while doing this.

F. Extra-Exciting Places

    If you believe Pines' hypothesis on arousal levels leading to love, you might try folk dancing, hiking or scary movies.

Events and places to avoid on first dates:

1. Weddings
2. New Year's Eve
3. Valentine's Day
4. Major holidays like Christmas
5. Family celebrations
6. Baptisms

    Tip for the guys: Before you pick up your date, be sure that you have already been to the ATM and have cash in your wallet, enough gas in the car and directions to where you're going. You don't want her thinking you're a deadbeat from the get-go.

4. Make an effort to look good.

    First impressions are important. Consumer research shows that we make a decision about whether to purchase an item in less than 15 seconds. Dress appropriately for the occasion, but put some effort into your grooming and thought into what you're wearing.

To attract men, I wear a perfume called "New Car Interior."
Rita Rudner

5. What to talk about.

It probably doesn't matter as long as it's genuine and polite. Be curious about the person across from you. And check the conversation flow. Are you doing all the talking or asking all the questions? What is the other person doing? Is it an even exchange of information?

Ask really good questions, and then notice the answers. Be genuinely curious and get outside of yourself. Check to see if the conversation flows back and forth and if there is equal sharing. Here's an example of good questions that are neutral in nature:

"Where are you originally from?" "What was it like growing up there?" "Where have you traveled?" "What did you learn?" Notice these are all "W" questions.

Ask questions, but don't make it into an employment interview. Relax. You're going to see this person three times. You don't have to know their life history on the first date. You don't have to make a snap yes-or-no decision.

Notice if the other person is doing all the talking and not validating the things you say. Does the conversation always go back to her? Are you getting the feeling that he is self-centered? Communication doesn't mean talking; it means **sharing**. Be on the lookout for red flags, warning signs that make it unsafe to open up to this person.

There are two different ways to listen to another person. The first way is called Level One where, on the surface, you are listening to someone else, but you are really in your own head deciding what you can say back to him, or you are making some sort of judgment about what he is saying.

Level Two is having a strong focus on everything she is saying without the internal chatter and without judgment. When she is finished making her point, you respond by validating what you heard her say, ask if you are correct and then give your response.

You get the idea. If you don't, buy *If*, by McFarlane and Saywell, which has a whole lot of great "Suppose" questions. Carry it with you, present it as this neat book you found, and just start going through it.

To be more conversational, women can also start reading the sports page and men, *People*.

6. What <u>not</u> to talk about.

Do you ever hear things you really wish you hadn't when you are first meeting and getting acquainted?

There are some conversational taboos when getting to know someone, and they are sex, your ex (husband, lover) and sex with your ex!

Don't tell it all right off the bat. Yes, we all long to be known. But only by the right person. Save all the juicy stuff and the skeletons in your closet until you know that someone really cares and will receive what you are saying in a loving, compassionate way. Trust is very important.

The *Marry Me* guys advise, "A small comment about an intimate act with a guy other than ourselves confirms and paints the one picture that we don't want in our minds—the picture of you with other guys. The clearer that picture gets the less of a chance he will marry you." This is enough to keep you in the "Good for now" girl list and out of the "Wife potential" category.

They go on to say

"During the third or fourth date women become a little more open with the conversation they have with a man, and sometimes they think it is safe to talk about past sexual experiences. You figure, 'what the hell?' If you tell the guy this story, he cannot marry you. Keep your racy stories to yourself. Don't say something that a man will never be able to get out of his mind. One wrong anecdote may damage or completely destroy your chances of long-term commitment and marriage."

Don't divulge about your recent medical history, Grandma's insanity, yearly sales' quotas, or astrological compatibility.

Don't discuss why you can't get over your last relationship either. That, as well as any childhood abuses you may have experienced, is between you and your counselor at this point. And, may I remind you, that you are not supposed to be in the Dating phase if you're still not over someone else? It's just a waste of time. Go back to Pre-Dating.

It's in your best interest not to discuss, complain or brag about how much money you make. Your income is nobody's business until you have a steady enough relationship that you are talking of marriage, and money doesn't matter.

Nobody likes a "name dropper." Name-droppers don't feel good enough about themselves and try to boost themselves by boasting of their relationship with someone else.

Refrain from talking about the details of your surgery, a root canal or all the medications you are taking. Genital warts, herpes—save for later. Other people like to see you as a healthy person from the start.

Now that I've mentioned the negative topics to avoid, I once again encourage you to stay on the positive side of topics of conversations.

A special warning for children of alcoholics.

Being careful of what is said in the beginning is particularly true for children of alcoholics. Their gas gauge only measures empty [not trusting], or full [totally trusting], with very little in between. With these children in particular, in order not to get hurt, it's important to put other markings on the gas gauge. In other words, "Chunk it down." Divulge a little at first, something that will not hurt you. Then see how it goes for awhile, meaning days and weeks and months. If you feel safe with this person having this information, chunk it down again, giving just a little more information over a period of many months. Stop. Take your time. See if it's safe. Keep chunking it down. Stop immediately if you feel uncomfortable. Find out why. Decide if your reasons are valid or not before giving up more of yourself.

This is the method children of alcoholics probably will have to use all of their lives. But it will
- Allow them to open up, begin to trust and eventually achieve intimacy and
- Keep them from becoming too vulnerable and open to being hurt.

6. What **not** to do on early dates.

Tom Wolfe, in *Hooking Up*, informs us that old meanings for getting to first, second, third base and home plate no longer apply. In today's world, the era of "hooking up," first base means deep kissing ("Tonsil hockey"), groping and fondling. Second base means oral sex. Third base means going all the way. And home plate means learning each other's name.

And since you have **boundaries, standards**, and **self-respect**, you are not going to do any of that. You will not have sex on your first date. All you would be doing is getting to know each other's bodies instead of each other's brains and hearts. Most men and women agree that sex is okay after three dates. Twenty-eight percent of men surveyed think that sex is okay after only one date. They're wrong.

The Six-Before-Sex Rule.

When we meet someone who attracts us, our physiology propels us into the mating dance. Lust is ultimately biochemical, driven by testosterone, neurohormones and other chemicals that interact to create sensations of desire, arousal and orgasm.

This dance consists of three separate stages. The first stage is Attraction. When we like someone, all kinds of hormones—norepinephrine, dopamine, testosterone, and estrogen—pump in. The chemicals act as a "Love Cocktail," nature's booster to get us together to procreate. It ensures survival of the species and all that stuff.

At this stage, if a brain scan were taken, it would show very little blood flowing to the neo-cortex, which is where we think. This means that in this initial stage, when the full sexual explosion kicks in, you can't think rationally. You don't even really know whom you're with.

So in order to preserve some kind of rational thought, I'd like you to forego having sex for at least six dates. Forget the meal-and-a-feel action.

Remember that I told you that I would protect you?

Well, this rule is one of the most important tools. It stops you from having sex with someone before you are ready. And it keeps you from hating yourself later for being such a fool, or so easy, or so misused. And, importantly, it keeps you from ending up with the wrong partner.

Because once the sexual dance begins, the entire flavor of the relationship is changed. Once you're locked onto this person **lustwise**, you're pretty much gone for the next 12 to 16 months, which is when the Love Cocktail wears off. You won't be attracted to another person while you're in the Attraction stage, and you won't listen to anything negative about your love-buddy. You just won't hear it. There's no blood going to the thinking brain!

Again, six dates is the **minimum** amount of time to be celibate. It could be longer if you feel that you are not a good judge of character or if you have been taken advantage of in the past. The point is to wait until you feel comfortable and you're thinking with your head as well as your hormones.

This rule particularly applies to men. I've worked with many male clients who immediately become sexually involved and smitten without really knowing their partner. They call when they've been going together for a while, she's starting to talk marriage and children, and he realizes that he doesn't even know if he really **likes** her!

Again, **caution!** When you get sexual, your mind goes away. So try to decide if the person fits your partner profile and is potentially a good match for a long-time partner **before** you jump into bed.

And to do this, wait at least six dates. Normal dates. One every few days, with space and thinking time in between. Four dates a day doesn't count. Don't be forced and don't be hurried and don't be fast-talked into doing something you don't want to. And even when you want to—wait at least six dates. Once you're sexually involved, it's much harder to get perspective and to extricate yourself if need be.

Sexual intimacy has very little to do with attractiveness and **everything** to do with emotional intimacy and trust. How long does **that** take?

Remember the "Coyote Ugly" joke? A man wakes up in bed, after a one-nighter, with his arm around a woman so ugly that instead of waking her, he gnaws off his arm! Keep in mind that you're not looking for someone to help you make it through one night but someone for a lifetime.

And women! You know you hate yourself and lose all self-esteem if you sleep with losers who want sex and then treat you poorly. Take the time to decide if the guy is someone you'd like to spend a lot of time with and whether he's sensitive to your feelings before you get your heart entangled. As E. Jean says in *Elle*, "Sex won't bring you love, it will bring you pleasure. Get that straight or men will play you for a fool the rest of your life."

I have worked with singles on both sides of the spectrum. One is the Audrey-Hepburn type I mentioned before. To her objection that men just wanted to have sex with her, I advised, "Just say no. Tell them you have a Six-Before-Sex Rule." "But won't that make them mad?" she asked. "Yes, if all they want is sex." By having a Six-Before-Sex rule, she can protect herself and not have sex until she is <u>ready</u>.

The other client was a man who loved having sex and was attractive enough that women came on to him all the time. But now he was interested in having a serious relationship and thought he had found the perfect woman. "What should I do?" he asked. "If you are serious about this woman, don't have sex with her until you really get to know her," I advised. "It's too easy for you to get caught up in good sex and then not develop the relationship. And then you get too far down the road because you're sexually committed, and you don't even know if you really like her or not." "But I like sex," he countered. "Then go have it with someone you know you're <u>not</u> seriously interested in," I suggested "and keep the Six-Before-Sex rule with this woman."

Whether you decide to wait six dates, ten dates or thirty dates, for the health of the relationship, get to be friends first, build a solid foundation of genuine liking, let the feelings and trust develop, **then** determine if you want the relationship to progress to a physical one. You want to be marriage material and not the good-for-now girl or boy. Remember: lust, not love, is blind.

Touching

If you feel comfortable and genuinely like the person, it conveys warmth to touch them on the arm or shoulder when appropriate. When you shake hands be sure to look them straight in the eye and smile. Make your handshake firm and sincere.

Don't go to either home until after the sixth date. Homes have bedrooms and nice comfy couches and may jump you ahead of the "Six-Before-Sex" rule. If you really, **really** like the person, and can't remember why the Six-Before-Sex rule is important, go back and re-read that section **now!** Continue to get to know your date better so you can make a good decision for yourself no matter how horny you might be.

Who pays?

Usually it's the guy. That's just the way it is. Certainly, in the beginning, the person who initiates pays, and, if you're reading along, it's the guy who initiates.

The end of the date

Everyone wants to know about kissing goodnight on the first date. There are different kinds of kisses with different meanings behind each one. There is a perfunctory "peck on the cheek" when friends meet; there is the warm, family quick lip kiss and then there is the romantic, lingering open mouth kiss. When first meeting and getting to know someone, it is safer to stay with a hug instead of kissing, until you know where you want that to lead. Do not kiss someone because you think they're expecting it or because you feel you should or have to. It's your body–you decide the level of affection.

You actually can tell a lot from the way a person kisses. If you decide that you would like to kiss your date romantically, then do it right. Lips should talk. They should explore. They should be soft and inquisitive rather than bold and assertive.

The women's lips should lead. Guys, women don't want to have to brace themselves to withstand the strength of your kiss. They also don't want stranger's tongues thrust down their throat.

Women are usually better kissers because they've been practicing since they were ten. If the guy's not a great kisser, see if he's willing to learn. As Mae West said, "I never met many great kissers but fortunately I had lots of time to teach them."

Saying goodnight

Here's how to interpret what you hear, according to The Advice Ladies:

- "I'll call you" means: "I'm standing here trying to say good-bye and I'm not sure I want to see you again and I don't want to hurt your feelings so I'll just say this!"
- "I'll call you soon" means when the moon is in the seventh house and Jupiter aligns with Mars.
- "I'll call you on Tuesday" means definitely within the next decade.
- "Would you like to have dinner next Tuesday? I'll call you tomorrow to confirm" means I want to have sex with you as soon as possible.

Ladies, stay cool. After the first date or even after the first couple of dates, don't ask him for any other date commitment, and don't plan his calendar. If you can't **be** cool, then **act** cool anyway! The old-fashioned "playing hard to get" is still in your best interest. Stay in your own life where you were before you met. Otherwise you look needy and desperate to a guy.

And guys, don't say you'll call if you have no intention of doing so.

Opportunity dances with those
who are already on the dance floor.
                    Speaker unknown

Three dates and they're out.

What if you, the woman, are not interested after the third date?

You must come up with a very firm, but polite, refusal. Never string someone along. What would being firm and polite sound like? An example: "I think you're a nice person, but I'm not really interested in pursuing a relationship with you." Period. If they persist, you can add, "I believe we have different values [or goals,] so I don't see it going anywhere." Period.

Short, sweet, and direct. What does it say about you if you dodge phone calls or have a friend tell the person you don't want to see them any more? Have the integrity to end it nicely.

If you, the man, the caller, are not interested, you can Lone-Ranger, with no goodbye and no answers, leaving her with no idea who you are.

But don't use excuses. Excuses hurt much worse than the honest truth does. But if your date hasn't read this book, and doesn't know not to call you at this point in the relationship—in other words, if she calls and asks you out—you may be direct, using the same response as above. Or you can be almost honest. For example, "You're a nice person, but I'm just too busy to pursue anything further."

If you are divorced.

Make negatives into positives. You now know what it takes. Because of your mistakes, you can bring more to the relationship. Treat the relationship as if it's your first. Make this new person the only one in your life. Don't talk about your ex, don't see your ex, and certainly don't compare your ex.

Single-parent dating

Being single with children is not easy, and it is especially not easy when it comes to dating. On the one hand, I suggest that you keep your children separate and apart from the person you are beginning to date for as long as possible. First of all, children always want to have their mommy and daddy together and so will be upset by a new person intruding. Secondly if your children are involved with people you date and it doesn't work out, then, to them, it seems like another divorce or rejection.

On the other hand, if you're dating someone with children, I feel that you should meet the children fairly early into the relationship because who wants to get involved with someone who has obnoxious children? As far as I'm concerned, obnoxious children are a deal-breaker and better to find out as soon as possible.

So my compromise suggestions are these:

If you like the person and think they could be a perfect partner, meet the children between the third and eighth date. Meet them casually, preferably at a large gathering, such as at a church service, a family picnic, or a mall. Just" happen" to run into them where they won't know that you're interested in their parent and are checking them out. If you subsequently go on and develop a relationship with the person, there will be plenty of time to do things as a family group. But not on the first dates.

Remember that you're just getting to know this person. You don't know yet if they're trustworthy. Will this lovely woman act like Maria Von Trapp or Sleeping Beauty's evil stepmother to your children? Will this handsome man be the supportive, loving father who will give your children a great life or will he be the boyfriend/stepfather that abuses your daughter(s) and fights for control with your son(s)?

With children in the picture, you really have to go slowly and you really have to get to know the person. If you're single without children, a mistake only hurts one person. When you're a parent, a mistake can have difficult and long-lasting consequences that keep multiplying.

Even at an early stage, do you want promises made to your child that will not be kept? If you hear, early in the dating relationship, "Let's take the kids to Disneyland or out to dinner," it is a gesture to get close to your kids and try to woo you through them. What happens to you and your children if the date changes their mind?

The following suggestions depend on whether the couples are 1. A single parent dating single people with no parental responsibilities or 2. Prospective couples where **both** are single parents with parental responsibilities.

Of the first set, the *Marry Me* guys comment that "Women with children. It's harder. Because the ex is always going to be around. The odds of getting married are better if you date men who already have children or older men who might love an instant family. Most single men put women with children into the 'good enough for now' category. Younger, never been married men are tough."

Of the second set, where both partners have children living with them, I would like to say that the Brady Bunch does not exist! Combining his and her children under one roof is one of the most difficult situations that a couple can face for many reasons:

1. Favoritism. Each parent is protective of his children's welfare and needs. It takes a mature and strong person to see all issues honestly and act accordingly.

2. Discipline. Each set of children was raised with different rules and standards. If one parent is lenient and the other has strict rules and boundaries, the leniently raised child is going to feel that he is being singled out and picked on when the rules tighten up. This child may resent the stepparent and their ways and feel unloved, uncared for, and not good enough. Conversely, the strictly raised child may feel lost and without structure. Thus starts chain reactions of behavior from the child(ren) and consequences from the parents that may lead to chaos.

3. Jealousy. At least one of the children's absent parents most likely will have visiting or co-parenting privileges. These children will be entertained separately from the others. Jealousy can occur when one set of kids is taken to better places and experiences more than the others.

Or one parent may simply be more demonstrative with his children than the others, and this also can lead to jealousy.

So…what's the bottom line on all this? The bottom line is that blending families is very, very hard. But then again, I'm from Santa Barbara. I know some families here that have three or four different genetic branches grafted onto their family tree. And all the ex's and step-kids and step-grandparents get along great. In fact they make it look like fun!

I'm not saying it can't be done. I'm just asking you, at this early stage, to be very particular. And very circumspect so that innocent children and **you** don't get hurt–now or later.

Handling rejection.

This is the worst part, isn't it? Being dumped. It's a totally demoralizing, terrible, awful, sickening, ego-degrading worst thing to happen, isn't it?

Yes. Being rejected can be a painful experience. That's why I've given you all this information–so you've kept your self-esteem high and haven't made yourself vulnerable to this kind of hurt.

And . . . no. As bad as it seems, rejection is not any worse than you make it out to be. You can choose to make it into a catastrophe or an "oh-well" experience.

The catastrophic approach is going to result in depression, anxiety, and feelings of hopelessness. In this mood, you can dwell in the land of "I'm never going to find anyone for me" as long as you want, but all it will do is make you miserable. It's certainly not going to attract a new Perfect Partner.

On the other hand, you could accept that it wasn't meant to be, believe there is a better fit out there for you and move on. With every relationship there is something for you to learn, either about yourself or about life. If you can find it in your heart to forgive the person who rejected you and forgive yourself, you will move through the pain better and faster and not carry the baggage on to the next person in your life.

Again, "It's not failure, it's feedback."

If you followed the Six-Before-Sex rule, you won't have sunk into the Attraction stage with someone unworthy of you.

And if you have your boundaries in place, you won't stay too long in a relationship that doesn't feel right to you anyway. These two tools should guard you from unexpected rejection.

Mark Victor Hanson, the co-author of the Chicken Soup series, said that they took their book to 103 publishers which all rejected it. The 104th one said yes. Think how much rejection that was, and yet they endured.

One of the truisms for a really good salesman is that if he never is rejected then he is not trying hard enough.

Remember, you are "filling the pipeline." A certain amount of sales isn't going to happen. If you can be philosophical about it rather than doomed, you'll be faster on your way to finding the Perfect Partner.

But sometimes this is hard to remember, especially when you're depressed. So I want you to cut out this card and keep it nearby—or even make copies of it for your mirror, bedside table, telephone stand and office—to get you past this hurdle.

I have been rejected. This could be for many reasons.

1. They are not ready for a committed relationship.
2. They have different values than I do.
3. They have different wants and needs than I do.

Even though I am alone again, I have learned from this relationship.

I will take what I have learned, that _____ _____ and use it to change_____..

Continued

> I am still a person of worth, of many wonderful characteristics, and I am lovable. And if I have done somethung to sabotage this situation, I will change my behavior by_____
> _____
> so I can learn and grow from this experience.
>
> I may go through many rejections, but this is just part of the process of meeting and getting to know more people. I will not take it personally. This rejection says more about the other person than it does about me. If they don't think I'm wonderful, then they are not the right person for me. Better to end it now so that I can begin again to look for the ideal partner that **is** out there.

The essence of co-creating a lifetime partnership is to:

Move slowly and spend **quality time** interacting. Build the relationship one brick at a time with as much honesty as is safe. Build it to last a lifetime. This is difficult when you are in the first six months of a new relationship and you have that lusty, "in love" feeling. It normally takes six months for the initial infatuation to even begin to subside. Then reality sets in and you see the other person for who they really are.

So . . . spend time to get to know the person and become friends first; stay out of bed; and let feelings and trust develop with time.

Overheard at Starbucks:

He: *You know, I'm finishing law school this year and I think it's time I settled down and got married. How would you feel about spending the rest of your life with me?*

She: *Frankly, I don't know if I can finish the evening.*

71

Chapter Three – Rating

After you've gone out for at least three dates it's time for a rating assessment. Nothing too complicated.

- Am I having a good time?
- Do I like myself when I'm with them?
- Do I feel respected, listened to, and attractive?
- Do I feel validated?
- Am I feeling nurtured in the relationship?
- Would Elaine consider him "Spongeworthy?"[1]
- Are their core values similar to mine?

---

[1] *Seinfeld, NBC Television.* Seinfeld's friend, Elaine, would really check out men because she only had a few of her favorite contraceptive sponges left, and she didn't want to waste them on just anyone.

Thoughts to remember:
- You don't have to, nor will you, fall in love with everyone you go out with. And vice versa. Don't take it personally.
- You don't have to think about marrying the person yet.
- You don't have to love someone just because they love you. (In fact, if they say they love you after three dates, suspect something's wrong.)
- You don't have to like everyone you love or love everyone you like.
- You don't have to do anything you don't want to, **especially** sexual acts.
- You don't have to rush into a relationship. (Are you at the sixth date yet?)
- You don't have to put up with any garbage.
- You don't have to heal or help others.
- For a long-term relationship, it's best to like the person before you love them.

So now . . . who would it be a good idea to reject at this point?

The story of the monkey and the snake.

A monkey and a snake live together on the edge of the jungle. One day the monkey sees that a log is about to fall and crush the snake. With heroic might, the monkey catches the log and saves the snake. At which point, the snake turns around and bites the monkey. With his dying breath, the monkey asks "But why?"

The snake replies, "What did you expect? It's in my nature."

So . . . reject all snakes.

Look carefully at people who <u>partially</u> meet the profile of what you want in a significant other. This is where you get stuck, where it's good but not good enough. Find out about the places where the person is out of sync with your profile. Determine if they are changeable- (But really, who ever changed someone else?) Do they have any characteristics or behaviors that you can't stand? Determine if they are as important to you as you first thought. Be tough in sticking to your standards, and don't waffle on this one. Do you want to be happy half the time but frustrated, angry and/or depressed the other half? I think **not**.

Lifetraps

What are Lifetraps? Lifetraps are a concept utilized by author and psychologist, Jeffrey Young, to explain behavior. Basically, they are the way we learn to perceive, think and act because of how we're parented. Lifetraps are really what they say - traps. For instance, if we're raised by parents who are fearful of bad things happening, we're going to register this in our minds and bodies. But we won't realize that we're doing this because we're children and don't know better. We might not learn that this is not normal parenting until we're much older. Or we may never know that we see the world as a more dangerous place than most people do.

Another example is being raised in a family where we always got our own way. We may be spoiled and insensitive to others. But we don't know that because we were taught that we were the most important thing in the world. And so selfish behavior just feels natural to us.

It takes much work and awareness to avoid falling into Lifetraps, mainly because they feel so comfortable. They're what we're used to . . . and blind to.

Consider <u>your</u> Lifetraps and what kind of partners they attract. A man who does not drink alcohol because of having had to deal with alcoholic parents can walk into a party and, out of hundreds of people, he will attract alcoholics. Why? How? It's his Lifetrap. And it feels so familiar to him that he won't realize that these partners can be deadly for him.

How to avoid this? Be aware. Here are some Lifetraps and the kind of partners they attract.

Abandonment: a partner may be involved in another relationship, emotionally unstable, a Peter Pan, or not consistently available. They may be ambivalent about you, wanting you but holding back.

Mistrust and abuse: The person has an explosive temper that is scary to you. They will put you down, making you feel worthless. They have no respect for your needs but will do anything to get their way. They may be a con artist in business and very often lose control when they drink.

Emotional deprivation: They don't listen to you and may do all the talking. They are cold and aloof, not comfortable with hugging and kissing. You always give more than you get.

Dependence: This person is like a father or mother figure, strong and protecting. They treat you like a child and do almost everything for you.

Subjugation: The partner is domineering and expects things to be their way. They have a very strong sense of themselves and become irritated or angry when you disagree. Or they may be easily hurt so that you feel you have to take care of them. They are not very competent, may be irresponsible, and become sad, worried or depressed easily. They are very needy and dependent on you.

You don't mean to have these Lifetraps. In fact, you'd rather not. Potential partners don't mean to hurt you. But . . . it's in their nature. Break free now before your Lifetrap puts you in a relationship trap.

If you fear you're falling into a Lifetrap, stop yourself and examine the dynamics of the situation more closely. This is the time **not** to follow your intuition. Keep talking, asking the questions, staying out of bed.

Reject members of 12-Step programs that haven't been clean for 12 months. They still have too much changing and getting straight to do. A relationship before that is not healthy for them or stable for you. Wait until you know what you're getting.

Expectations

Some of your standards and expectations might need to change. Sure you'd like to date Tom Cruise, Ben Aflleck, Madonna, George Clooney or Shania Twain! How realistic is this? Good men and women are hard to find. So you might have to cut down your "No Way" list. A person's appearance and manners can be changed. Find your diamond in the rough and then polish it. Easier than catching Benicio del Toro's eye after he's already been discovered.

Marsha Wayne

Values

Have you ever met someone you really like yet makes you feel uncomfortable? This might be your different values bumping up against each other. It's the Core Values match that is important. Ask your date what their values are. Write down your plan here.

- What are their Values?

- What ones are similar to yours?

- Which ones do you have trouble with?

- What are you going to do about these?

- How can these hurt you?

- Are you prepared for this kind of hurt?

- If not, what are you going to do?

Take time and figure these out **now**. Remember, I'm protecting you from getting lost in dead-end relationships. Do this exercise right now before you go any farther. Let's make sure your head is working as well as your heart.

If love is the answer, could you please rephrase the question?
Lili Tomlin

Getting your needs met.

Meanwhile, as you continue to date and explore, make sure your own needs are being met.

- Are you educating your partner on how to treat you so that you feel loved?
- Have you given up your life for theirs?
- Are you taking care of your own needs or are you depending on your partner to fill you up?
- Have you abandoned all your other friends?

You created a good life before you met. Why would you give it up?

Some caveats at this point:

Fear of intimacy.

If you're wondering if there's a still better partner out there, sit down and have a heart-to-heart with yourself. Is this about the person not meeting your ideal expectations or is it about your getting nervous as you grow closer? Intimacy is difficult for people who were abused, emotionally deprived, abandoned, or who are children of alcoholics. So have a soul-searching discussion and figure out what it is. Because if it's fear of intimacy, it's not going to get better. The particular person doesn't matter. It's mainly **you**.

If the problem is you, here's the solution. You "chunk it down". (Remember this from Chapter Two?) That means you take little baby steps, one at a time. The types of people who experienced the kinds of childhood traumas mentioned above tend to be all-or-nothing types. They either will not thaw at all, or they will roll over on their backs and worship their partner as a God or Goddess. So instead, follow this program:

1. Open up a tiny bit, a bit that you will feel comfortable about exposing even if the person is a lout. Then wait. Days. Weeks. Months. Test. See how it goes.
2. If you still feel safe and secure, divulge a little bit more. Repeat the wait-and-see procedure.
3. Keep "chunking it down."
4. Go as far as you feel comfortable. If you feel vulnerable, compromised or betrayed, **stop**. Don't go any farther.

The "chunk-it-down" rule is a lot like the Six-Before-Sex Rule. Protect yourself emotionally by not going faster than is safe for you. Speed is not of the essence here. Your safety and your comfort are what matter. Let your head, not you heart or hormones, rule at this point.

Fear of assertiveness.

Sure you want that other person to really like you. That's the point. You want them to like you, not some person who agrees about everything. This is the time to be honest, to have an opinion and say what you like, don't like, prefer, couldn't care less about, etc.

Educate your partner on how to treat you. How do you do this? Stand up for yourself and speak out. If what you hear hurts you, say, "That hurt me. Please don't say that anymore." If something offends you, say, "That offends me. Please don't do that around me again."

As you're getting to know someone, be honest. It will not only help you get what you want, but it will let you find out at an early stage if they are willing to listen to you and provide what you need. Again, better to learn sooner and have the time available to look for a more compatible partner than to linger in something that ultimately is not going to work.

For women, this assertiveness is like taking a breast cancer exam. No one wants to find out they have breast cancer. So many women just don't do the exam. But you have cancer whether you examine or not. <u>And</u> if you catch it early, you can do something about it.

Again, the snake has its nature whether you ask about it or not. So <u>ask</u>.

Single-parent rating assessment

As I mentioned in the Dating chapter, once children are involved—his, hers, or both—like Rick in *Casablanca*, you're "going to have to do the thinking for the [bunch] of [you]." So think hard. And throw away the rose-colored glasses. Here are some questions to ask:

1. How do I really feel about this person's child(ren)?
2. How do I feel about how this person interacts with my child(ren)?
3. Would we share similar values as a family?
4. Do we have similar goals for our child(ren)?
5. Do I like their parenting style? Discipline style?
6. Would I trust this person alone with my child(ren)? Is there any evidence that this person might be abusive to my child(ren)?
7. Could I entrust my children's long-term care to this person if something happened to me?
8. Would there be an equal distribution of money and labor in caring for these children?
9. Would the children truly become "ours" or theirs only or mine only?

10. What kind of influence will their child(ren) have on mine?
11. Do I think that if I married this person and/or blended our families that the happiness would outweigh the difficulties?
12. Am I consenting to be with this person because I truly like/love them or because I need a parent for my children?
13. Would I be considering this person as a potential partner if it weren't for my child(ren)?

If you have a negative answer to any of these questions, **stop**. Do not go any farther. This is not the right situation for you. Stop kidding yourself. Slow down and ask some more questions if you want, but it probably won't help. Your intuition should be on red alert right now, practically screaming to you to let go. Listen to it. Let go.

If, however, you both have positive thoughts and feelings and can predict that being together will be a healthy step for everyone involved, then it's time to **slowly** start including the children in your plans.

Start by having each person spend more time with the other's family. If that works well, and there are no changes to your answers above, then slowly combine the sets.

Do so with a kind heart and a sense of humor. And remember that the flexible branch survives the storm.

Time-out for older singles

Studies have shown that many women who are in their fifties are not interested in re-marrying. Most women have been married at least once, and many of them have lived alone for a while. And they find they like their freedom. They don't want to be "a nurse and a purse."

In contrast, men who are this age or older are very interested in re-marrying or at least re-coupling. Most men admit they do not do well on their own. They need someone to run their social life, make sure they are eating healthily, sleeping right and taking care of themselves. For men in their fifties and older, getting married is a wonderful idea and even can extend their life expectancy.

But women need to think long and hard before going into a relationship. If you're a fiftyish female, most of your marital candidates will be 50 to 70 years old. (That is unless you want a "boy-toy." You go, girl!)

A man's health, statistically, deteriorates at a younger age than a woman's does. Chances are that in the next ten years, the now 60-70-year-old man will have some major health problems and/or be an invalid. Is this what you're looking for? To possibly be a major caretaker for an elderly, sick man?

I raise the question because some of my middle-aged, single, female clients have ended up in this position, and they **hate** it.

And they even considered that this could happen at the time they got married. But they put on their rose-colored glasses and decided that it wouldn't happen to **them**, and, even if it did, it was worth the good years they would have together. Now many say how much they regret their decision. And how they would give **anything** to get out of the situation. But how do you leave a sick shut-in who can't hear or has no balance or needs help with his medications or requires someone to drive him around?

Red flag, red flag! Really assess the pros and cons of this situation. Write yourself a worst-case scenario and be unflinching in your rating of how you would like this. Love, and the attraction stage, can take away your rationality and judgment, so cold-bloodedly consider the future. How **much** older is this man? What is his health like generally? How will you feel if you become a stay-at-home caretaker?

And, having considered all of this, are you still willing to say yes to "For better or for worse" and "In sickness and in health?"

If the answer is Yes, you are willing to take the risk, where should you look? Have you ever considered tracking down an old flame? Many people have, with positive results. Obstacles that might have kept you apart when you were younger—sexual mores, distance, and different interests or values—may no longer be relevant. Research by psychologist Nancy Kalish shows that of 1,000 couples who re-met (and presumably re-coupled) after being apart for five years or more, 72% are still together, one for over 50 years.

How to find these classmates? Try the alumni office of your old school. Or use a reunion site like classmate.com, alumni.net or gradfinder.com. Or if you're really interested, Ussearch.com will conduct various searches for $39.95 to $59.95.

Rating Assessment.

Having read through the previous material, where are you now? Check Your True Statements:

☐ I recognize quickly the types of partners I used to be attracted to and I know my own Lifetraps

☐ I acknowledge this attraction as nothing more than conditioning from my past

☐ I recognize truly available people

☐ I recognize people who will listen to me and honor me

☐ I recognize people who are in a process of growth

☐ I see people for who they are rather than for who I want them to be

☐ I am attracted to partners that are good for me

☐ I surround myself with people whose core values are similar to mine

☐ I am not afraid to speak up for what I want

Count your Trues. If your score is less than five, reread the information and ask yourself if you need to **stop** and do more work on your Lifetrap or Pre-Dating issues. Don't keep finding the wrong people over and over again. Invest the time to get straight with yourself rather than corralling the wrong doggies.

If it looks like this could be a possible life partner, and you've had the minimum six dates, its time to think about having sex.

Sex appeal is 50 percent what you've got,
And 50 percent what people think you've got.
Sophia Loren

Sex.

Remember that once you have sex with this person, your mind is going to be on vacation for a year. If you're ready, here are some tips for sex.

1.Discuss any sexually transmitted diseases, not just AIDS but things like genital warts and Herpes. As much as you might want to have this person as your partner, and are afraid of losing them if you are honest, it's not fair to be anything but 100% truthful about a disease that might effect their future. Do not decide to wait and confess later, when they're hooked. That's a definite no-no. They will probably hate you for it and what you've exposed them to. Say it before.

2. If you want them to be committed before you have sex with them, tell them. I personally think that some sex before committing to monogamy is a fair deal. Most men start calling a woman their girlfriend after the tenth date. So somewhere between the sixth and tenth date, you might want to have uncommitted sex and see what it's like with this person. If it is good or at least something workable, get the commitment to monogamy. If it's not great or you get bad vibes from it, you can put off committing until you have more information and are sure.

Exactly what does commitment entail? Does it include the other person staying out of strip joints, not viewing pornography, not seeing people of the other sex without your knowing about it, and/or not corresponding with past partners on the Internet? The answer to all of these should be yes. You're looking for a committed relationship that will lead to marriage.

All the behavior above takes the person out of commitment. It's the third leg of the stool that can keep a bad relationship from crashing because it provides a sexual and or emotional outlet, an alternative to seeing if you and your partner can balance as a couple.

To have <u>great</u> sex, ultimately, there needs to be an understanding that the relationship is monogamous, strong and in good health. In order to attain the type of intimacy that great sex requires, trust and security are essential.

3. Communicate your likes and dislikes in a loving and considerate manner. Sure, the sex in the beginning should be fantastic with all that testosterone going. But in order to sustain healthy enjoyment, you must communicate how much you like or dislike a particular action or activity.

This doesn't mean you need to be a traffic cop. Yes, no. More, less. Higher, lower. That takes all the pleasure and spontaneity out of it for the other person. Suggest one thing during lovemaking every couple of times. Then lie back and communicate your pleasure when your partner gets it right.

You can even talk about what was great after the sex, but don't turn into an analyst about it.

4. Stay physically fit.
Supposedly people who work out on a regular basis have better sex. Exercise increases flexibility, stamina, and strength, all of which contribute to vital, sustained pleasure.

That may be so, but my feeling is that the more you like your body, the better the sex is. Some people work out a lot because they are terribly insecure about their physique, and this will <u>negatively</u> affect their sexuality,

So, attain a level of fitness that makes you like yourself, and then don't be reluctant to share your body with someone else.

5. Don't be ashamed or embarrassed.

Eventually, you want sex to be extremely pleasurable. That doesn't mean you have to ask for it all right away. Ease into it. Remember, good sex is about developing trust.

If there's something you particularly like, don't be afraid to ask for it. Why not explore the full realm of your sexual pleasures?

On the other hand, if what you're asking is outside of your partner's sexual repertoire, don't push. You don't have to have everything you'd like to make the sex great.

If you are concerned about how your partner may react to a fantasy you have, first discuss how they feel about fantasies in general. If they're somewhat open to them, then start with the least scary. Usually men have more fantasy thoughts and nothing will faze them.

If you don't like your partner's fantasy, by all means say no. Whips and black leather are certainly not everyone's cup of tea. Don't be afraid of being labeled as prudish or icy if this is what you truly feel. But you might want to assess where your judgments on what's right and what's wrong came from. Who told you they were wrong? And are they a good judge of behavior?

If it doesn't offend you, "Allowing a man to indulge in his fantasies or merely act them out with

It's been so log since I made love,
I can't even remember who gets tied up.
Joan Rivers

you," according to the *Marry Me* guys, "is a surefire way of attaching yourself to him for life. When a man shares his sexual fantasies with you, he is giving you the chance of being his 'Dream' in bed. If you hear what he says and expound on the concept, he will never let you go."

6. Enjoy yourself.

Sexual intimacy is one of the greatest pleasures of being human. Understand that it is meant to be enjoyed and then, enjoy it. No one wants a partner who is simply going through the motions.

Part of enjoying, however, means **never** doing anything you don't want to do. If missionary-style sex is about as daring as you get, that's fine. Do not, repeat, do not get squeezed into doing something that is outside your moral and/or ethical boundaries. It's all right to be a "square," a "prude," a "tight ass," etc. etc. Not everyone keeps *Bridget Jones' Diary*. If you don't like it and don't want it, that should be the end of it. If your partner keeps pushing for something outside your comfort zone, they may be the wrong person for you. If hot sex is the main thing on their mind, beware! Remember, "To thine own self be true."

In addition to the general guidelines above, here's some specific advice on sexuality.

- Never talk about the size of a man's penis. You'll lose him. Men are too concerned already about size. He'll think he can't satisfy you.

If sex is such a natural phenomenon, how come there are so many books on how to do it?
Bette Midler

- Likewise, don't compare women's parts.
- Don't tell about all your sexual playmates.
- Ladies, never, ever have sex in a threesome. The man might love it at the time, but later he'll put you into the "Good for now" category.

Women, the *Marry Me* men have a formula for determining how many men you've slept with. Take the number of years over 16 that you are; multiply by 12; take that number and divide by 21. If the total exceeds 10, then cap the guys you have slept with at 10. " No man likes to think of his woman sleeping with another guy, much less ten other guys."

The *Marry Me* men are from the East coast. I'm from California. I'm not sure the same rule applies out here. I'm not sure anyone even cares about the number of sexual partners someone else has had. But I include their words of advise as another opinion. You can accept or reject them as you please.

If the sex is not going well, don't presume it's you. According to *USA Today*, there are many events or stressors that detract from your sex life.

Stress Detracts from Sex Life
Men and Women rank the top bedroom distractions

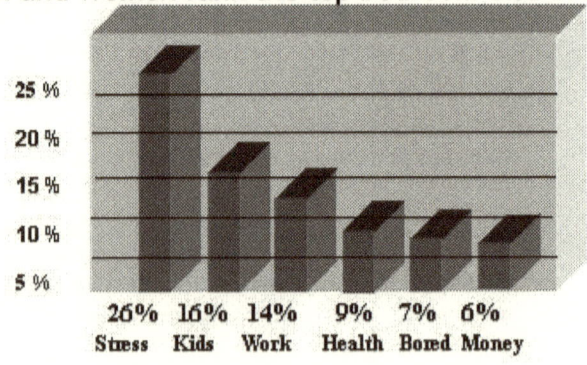

| 26% | 16% | 14% | 9% | 7% | 6% |
| Stress | Kids | Work | Health | Bored | Money |

You must make sex and intimacy a priority. Yes, in the beginning, you'll do it anywhere and everywhere, and you won't be able to get enough of each other. But around the year to year-and-a-half date the "Love Cocktail" wears off. The Attraction stage changes to the Attachment stage where the "tend and befriend" hormone of oxytocin becomes pre-eminent.

If you are a man who dates someone for a year or two and then gets bored and goes on to the next woman, realize that you are being ruled by your chemistry. Accept that there's more to being a couple than the lust, do yourself and others a favor, and grow into a more mature relationship.

This means that when the instant lust disappears you must plan so that you have ample time and space to allow the sex to be an important part of your lives.

If everything is going really well <u>except</u> for the sex, invest in seeing a therapist or licensed sex therapist. Don't let a trauma from the past deprive you of having enjoyment from your body <u>now</u>. To do so is a double insult to yourself. Therapists are trained to correct any dysfunction in a discreet, clinical, non-sexual way. This is their business. They're not going to be embarrassed so don't you be.

Still, all this having been said, remember that sex is only a part of the relationship. Leo Buscaglia, love expert, reminds us that in a poll of what's important in a relationship, sex ranks seventh.

> *Personally I know nothing about sex,*
> *because I have always been married.*
> *Zsa Zsa Gabor*

A last look

Don't fall into the commitment trap, which means being exclusive, until you're sure you're ready. And even when you choose to be exclusive, don't hibernate. Be out with other people and try to keep your life normal. Be open to your friend's opinions about your new partner. They might have the clarity that you now lack.

But sometime between the sixth date and the first year of dating, you'll hopefully reach a time where both of you are happy in the relationship, the sex is good, and the signs are pointing to monogamy. What next?

Time for a last look at what may be unhealthy before committing to a monogamous relationship and falling into love.

Here are the **intuitive signs** that something's wrong:

- You get physical symptoms when you are with this person (knot in your stomach, upset stomach, headaches, nausea, asthma, hives)
- You waste a lot of mental energy trying to figure out what is really going on in the relationship
- You don't trust them
- You feel intense jealousy
- You feel unsafe and unsure
- You feel "caged in"
- You feel bad more than you feel good
- You feel you are getting little in return for your investment
- You feel like you have no control over the relationship
- Something about them or the relationship just doesn't feel right
- Your "little voice" inside is screaming at you and you don't like what you hear

Here are the **behavioral signs,** the Actions and the Reactions, that are Red Flags:

- There is an unequal distribution of emotional and/or financial burdens or responsibilities to maintain the relationship
- You spend most of your time within their environment, like watching football games all the time, going to football parties (and you don't even **like** football) and spend little time alone together
- They lie to you
- There are frequent overly emotional scenes (crying, yelling, tantrums, threats, drama)
- They abuse alcohol or drugs and/or are addicted to sex
- They display any kind of violent or abusive behavior (including verbal and mental abuse)
- You never do anything without the other
- You are forced to do or say things that are not comfortable for you
- They withhold affection (hugs, kisses, support)
- They want more of your time and/or emotions than you are willing or able to give

If you checked off <u>even one</u> of these items, you could be in an unhealthy relationship. **Get help** or **get out** before it is too late. **Believe the little voice within telling you what you may not want to hear.** Listen to your heart–not your needs. Really. I told you I would help you and protect you, remember? This is not the time to gloss over any kind of bad sign. You're about to give your heart, time and feelings away. Are you sure you're ready? Better to get out now if it's wrong than ride a horse down a blind canyon that leads to nowhere. On the other hand, if everything feels and looks right then . . .

Relax and enjoy the ride.

If you think you've found the perfect love of your life, then take it easy and enjoy the ride. Make time to get to know each other during your first year together.

Women, if your biological clocks are ticking, unwind them. Relationships that start on the fast track usually die on the fast track.

Also, the *Marry Me* authors warn:

> All men do want to get married but they will be very careful about whom they select and they will usually take their time moving a relationship with her towards commitment. A man wants a continuation of what's already good. He doesn't want relationship talk, or reminders that he can't be with other women, no pressure. Don't talk about the two of you every time you get together. Never bring up the 'M' word—Marriage–in the first year of dating.

Don't play games with your potential mate. Be authentic. Be honest. Return phone calls. Don't say you're busy when you're not. Don't try to keep the person on a string. Work at coming together. A strong successful relationship is two healthy **"I's"** coming together as **"We."**

Put your needs behind you, or have them taken care of automatically by systems you have in place. Then enjoy the flight into the world of loving. You may never again have this freedom to give yourself over to being so completely in love.

Was that cannon fire, or is it my heart pounding?
Ingrid Bergman to Humphrey Bogart in "Casablanca"

 **Chapter Four – Mating**

You have just spent almost a year getting to know your committed partner. You have enjoyed a period of freedom and discovery, and, hopefully, been having a wonderful time. You have stayed in the moment. There has been no discussion of marriage or pressure to make the relationship legal.

Now, on schedule, at the one-year mark in your committed relationship, what comes next?

I believe that shortly after your one-year anniversary you should broach the subject of marriage. Marriage is the next logical step. You've had a chance to know and love each other.

Even if one partner is not ready for marriage because of education, job, children, or money commitments, these delays must be discussed. You need to have a map of what lies ahead. You have to agree that you want to **marry** and spend your lives together.

If you or your partner are not willing to commit to this, find out why. If the partner is unsure, what will make her sure? If he needs more time, how much? Pin this relationship down.

If there are still unexplainable obstacles or if something invisible is getting in the way, see the rest of the chapter for ideas on what might be blindsiding you and how to resolve the problems.

If, however, there are no rational problems, reasons, or obstacles, and your partner still won't commit to marriage, then **make the decision to get out**.

I know. You don't want to. You've invested so much time and energy and your **soul** in this relationship. You **love** them. You can't give it up—yet. And **yet** . . . yets turn into yesterdays quickly. Pretty soon, it's another year, then another, and then you've invested four years of your life, and you still don't have total commitment. Is this what you want? **Get Out!**

It doesn't matter if the projected marriage date is six months, a year, or two years out, as long as you have it.

Many couples are delaying their marriages. The average American engagement has stretched to 16 months, up from 11 months in 1990, according to the Conde Nast *Bridal Infobank*. This is due to couples marrying later and wanting a personalized wedding and being willing to wait for the right destination, photographer, season, honeymoon spot, etc. Also, because more couples are living together, there doesn't seen to be as much hurry. Finally, many thirty and older couples are now paying for their own weddings, and it takes time to save up for the event.

But even if you decide to postpone the wedding for three years, pick a definite date and start referring to each other as fiancé, fiancée. And, if you're a woman, have an engagement ring on your finger or a wedding date set.

Then, and only then, make the commitment to move in together. Again, this is the next logical step. You don't want to give up your life—and your apartment—without knowing where you're going. Remember, a dream without a plan is a mirage.

Below is my proposed time-line. Use it as a guideline. But realize at the two-year point at the maximum, if there's not a committed date, it's time to give up the relationship and start over. Appreciate everything you've learned from this partner, and move on.

From Pre-Dating to Marrying Time Line

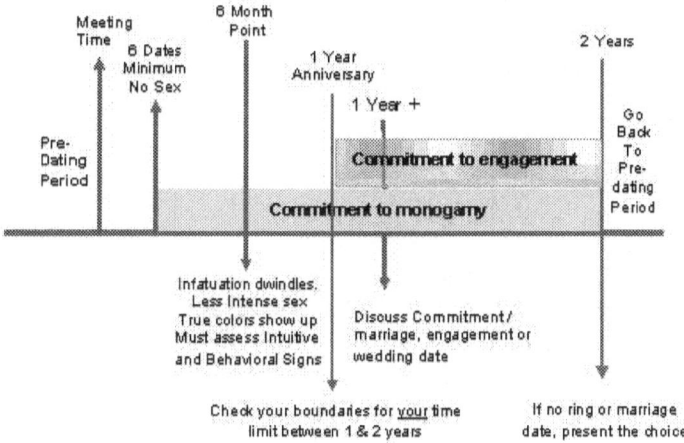

A **pre-committed couple** is one that hasn't made the commitment to monogamy and is still wondering, "Could this be the one?" Pre-commitment is the stage before becoming an exclusive dating couple and making an explicit commitment to be monogamous.

A **committed** couple has performed some identifiable act to become committed, usually with the intention of staying together until they decide to get married. The commitment is explicit, they've talked about what commitment means to both of them, and unhappiness alone is not a good reason to leave the relationship.

Going from uncommitted to marriage is usually a gradual process, starting with the first meeting and proceeding to the first date, planning future dates, spending time and money together, becoming exclusive, meeting each other's families, spending the week-ends together and moving in together.

Again this should happen in a gradual relaxed way. Couples who commit too soon may have only known each other for a couple of months, yet they've closed the pipeline. They have premature conjugation.

Couples where one person is committed and the other is not are not committed. If she's not ready to go there, he shouldn't either.

The key moments are:

- The 6-month point. Make the assessments to decide whether to proceed or find someone else.
- The 1-year anniversary. Don't talk about marriage before this. It's too soon. It takes this long to really get to know someone.
- Right after the 1-year anniversary. It's time to talk about the future: plans, engagement, and marriage.

- The 2-year anniversary. This is absolutely the maximum time to stay in this relationship without commitment to marriage. Give the partner a choice: Plan now or I'm gone.

Even after you're in a committed relationship, some are more apt to work and endure, to make it, than others. You've found the perfect relationship: now you've got to maintain it. Here are ways to make the relationship **better** with the partner you've assessed as perfect for you.

Move in together.

Again, at this stage, you're really liking your potential mate and thinking they might be The One. You know you're in love. You've been together for about a year. You've broached the possibility of getting married if things continue to go well. You are in a monogamous and committed relationship.

Now is the time to move in together. Living apart should not make the heart grow fonder. But it may lead to an artificial build-up of unfulfilled desire. Don't let sex, lust, be the reason you get married. The perfect relationship is built on values and interests, remember?

Moving in is taking one step at a time and trying it out. Remember "chunking it down?"

Yes I know it's a risk, but it's less risky than **not** trying it out before you commit to a lifetime of fidelity.

As for the "Free milk" analogy: Today, men are offered free milk any day of the week **without** any commitment. Living with someone complicates a man's life. He has to make changes and give up his independence. It's not about getting milk for free. Moving in is a step toward commitment.

Moving in with a man can complicate a **woman's** life as well. Before moving in with a partner, it is in your best interest, ladies, to first have a ring on your finger or a wedding date set. If that hasn't happened, at least make sure you've discussed marriage and a time frame. And that you've announced your engagement to your families and friends. Only then, move in together.

If one partner is not willing to go this far, **don't move in.** It is too soon. Someone can get hurt. Probably **you.**

If you feel protected, comfortable, and directed toward marriage, move in. It's the last chance to really sample before you buy.

If the closer you get and the more all aspects of your life entwine the **worse** it seems to get, there are still some areas that might need to be explored.

Five obstacles to commitment

1. High anxiety

Your partner might just be **anxious** about making such a big commitment and/or not used to spending so much time with one person. Give each other lots of space and privacy if one seems to crave it.

2. Your parents or their parents have been **divorced**. According to research by divorce expert Judith Wallerstein:

- Children of divorce can be gun-shy. They may have seen marriage at its worst.
- They don't like conflict. "They are uncomfortable around turmoil if their parents fought in front of them, and even the slightest altercation may send them running. They make terrible errors of judgment in whom they choose. They believe that marriage is

either a fairy tale, a wonderland [with high expectations] or worth nothing."

- Divorce can create jittery, idealistic children who will hold out for the perfect mate. Then because their expectations are so high, they will be disillusioned. Statistically, children of divorce marry later but divorce more often.
- Dating and courtship raise their hopes sky-high of being loved but also their fears of being hurt, abandoned and rejected. This amalgam of fear and loneliness can lead to multiple affairs, hasty marriages, early divorce and a second and third round of the same.
- They feel failure is inevitable.

Wow! A pretty grim picture! I remind you that this is one woman's findings. My purpose in including them is not to dishearten you but to make you aware of some of the undercurrents that may be circulating below the surface in your relationship if one or both of you are children of divorce. You may notice all, some or none of these characteristics in yourself or your partner.

Some therapists disagree with Wallerstein's findings. Divorced psychotherapist Chris Frey states that " Children of divorce are wounded, not damaged; wounds can heal. " Another divorce researcher, E. Mavis Hetherington says that 80% of children of divorce bounce back from the split within two years.

Whichever turns out to be factual, if you or your intended is a product of divorce, you must discuss the ramifications. Find out the level of trauma you or they suffered from the divorce and the extent of the residual scarring. Address how it affects your relationship and how you will deal with it.

3. Dysfunctional families

In a recent study in the *Journal of Personality and Psychology*, researchers at Penn State found that parents who are jealous, moody, volatile, critical or prone to dominate their spouse have a far worse effect on their child's future marriage than parents who divorce.

4. Your parents or their parents are **alcoholics.**

Children of alcoholics are afraid of intimacy. And why not? It was unsafe to be close to a mother or father who was inconsistent with their love and behavior or who became belligerent when drinking. If you cared too much, you got hurt.

These children tend to flee as the situation becomes more intimate. They are afraid to share their feelings, thoughts, and emotions. It's not safe.

Many of these children of alcoholics confuse intimacy with sexuality. They may believe that sex is all they have to share or that sex is all that someone wants. Some believe that the only way to achieve intimacy is through sex.

The best way to help yourself or someone else achieve intimacy is to go slowly. They need to be able to trust you a little bit, to open up and share just a little bit, and see if it's safe.

This is so important. When children of alcoholics decide they can trust someone, they sometimes completely let down their guard. They reveal everything, stripping themselves emotionally naked. They go too far too quickly. Often they will be hurt, betrayed, or disappointed. Again, patience is necessary. Don't make yourself vulnerable. In Adult Children of Alcoholics (ACA), they call it "chunking it down." Remember this? Share a little bit; check to see if that was safe; if so, share a little more; if not, close it down. Decrease your likelihood of being hurt. And minimize the fear of rejection by only sharing a small part at a time.

5. Commitment phobia

To a woman, a commitment is a pledge or a promise to do something. To a man with fear of commitment, it's the official consignment to prison, a mental hospital or boot camp.

For a man, fear of commitment is really more a fear of failure. Some young men are reluctant to marry because just living with a woman is easier. Their careers come first. They fear the cost of a divorce. They're not thrilled about sharing parenting chores. These men are not good candidates for today's egalitarian marriages.

So help him out. Talk about his fears; commiserate with him. Don't take it personally. It's really his issue, not yours. Try to encourage him over the hump, to accept some risk. Again, detach; <u>it's not about you</u>. Give him assurance about how right the two of you are rather than feeling hurt.

Without pushing, prodding or bugging, help him see the future: What you'll do together, how you'll feel. Help him roll the movie of his ideal life . . . with you sharing it. Help him get used to how nice it would be.

Work with him, but don't force him to commit. Just gauge whether he is committed. Usually if he's there, he's committed. Forcing him may kill the natural commitment that's present.

According to the *Marry Me* men,

If your man has not initiated the marriage conversation by your one-year anniversary then you should bring it up. Most men are thinking about marrying the woman they have dated for one year. The worst thing you can do is force your guy into a corner and tell him either to commit to marrying you or else. If you give him an ultimatum, he will think that you are trying to control him. Never actually use the marriage word. Tell him instead how much you care about him, how he has made your life better, and how you enjoy spending time with him. After he says he feels the same, then continue by telling him how compatible you think you are and how you could have a wonderful future before you. If he doesn't respond ask him "What do you think?" If he still doesn't tell you that he has a future with you, he is not interested in marrying you and you should leave him. If he responds positively, then and only then can you say, "When you say a future, does that mean marriage some day?" If he responds positively, you should **stop**. Don't push any further at this time.

He will love you more and want to marry you sooner if you don't give him ultimatums or pressure him into marriage.

Again, I have some ideas of my own about this. What the *Marry Me* authors might call an ultimatum, I would call a boundary. So I encourage you to check your boundaries around time frames and be firm with them. If your boundary is "I'll date someone for two years, and if there's no commitment by then, I'll leave," then honor your promise to yourself.

Place your bet on someone there all the time (while protesting that she's not ready to commit) rather than someone who pledges undying love but is seldom around.

Having thought through these different obstacles, you are ready to assess where you are in your relationship.

Assessment
How ready are you to be engaged?
Rate these statements on a scale of 1 to 10.

____My partner and I enjoy the same things and have very similar values.

____We communicate in a respectful manner.

____I feel comfortable with my partner's background and past.

____My partner treats me well.

____I have not noticed any major hurdles that would keep me from proceeding with this relationship.

____I am not overlooking, using rose-colored glasses, or in denial on any parts of their profile that don't fit my ideal partner profile.

____We compromise and are able to honor each other's goals.

____I am satisfied with the level of passion and intimacy between us.

_____I am my authentic self in this relationship.

_____I feel supported, honored and loved.

_____ **TOTAL**

> If you scored 85 to 100, proceed. If 70 to 85, check out the areas that don't feel right. If 55 to 70, is this really the right person for you? Less than 50? Time to recycle.

Single-parent mating assessment

If you are a single parent considering mating with a single person or with another single parent [either with or without parental responsibilities], add these questions:

_____Do my children want me to marry this person?

_____Would they give their permission?

_____Would they give their blessing?

_____If my partner has children, do they want him/her to marry me?

_____If my partner has children, do they accept me wholeheartedly?

_____Do I really like these children?

_____Are my children hurt in any way if we join together?

_____Do I have the ability and the desire to act as a parent to (more) children?

_____Do I have the ability and the desire to act as a parent to **these** children?

_____Do I have the emotional reserves to take on (more) children? Do I want to? What changes will I have to make in my life to do so?

_____Will I be required to be responsible for the financial welfare of children not my own?

_____Is adoption a consideration?

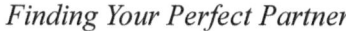

_____What will be my role with these other children? Or, what do I want my partner's role to be with my child(ren)? A friend, a babysitter, a guest, a full-on parent?

_____How will decisions be made about the children? i.e., I decide for my child(ren), they decide for theirs, or we decide everything together?

I could go on. But answering these questions honestly will give you a place to start. If you have any hesitations, don't proceed to marriage. Not even to moving in together. Many studies have shown how hard step-parenting is. Some couples I know have waited until the children have left the home before marrying, finding the combining of families too difficult.

I hope these questions will help you make your decision(s.) In any case, I recommend that if you decide to go ahead and blend your families, you get some family counseling before doing so.

Falling in love by design

Recently, Robert Epstein, former editor of *Psychology Today,* invited women to participate in an experiment to see whether a couple could **deliberately** fall in love. He would pick one woman and they would **learn** to love each other.

He wanted a woman who would forsake dating others for a period of months; would undergo intensive couple's counseling; would read books about love; and would sign a love contract pledging the two would systematically try to fall in love.

He explains that the way we seek a partner in America doesn't work because we are stuck in a myth of "living happily ever after."

Epstein believes that learning to love someone requires three pillars of support: psychological intimacy, relationship skills, and realistic expectations.

In order to give you the knowledge that Epstein feels is essential in learning love, let's look at the current thinking and technology on how to love.

Examining what historically doesn't work in marriage

Yes, some marriages work better than others and some are doomed from the beginning. Most can be improved. John Gottman, the modern-day American marriage guru, states that most problems in marriages never get solved; that when you get married you select your <u>irresolvable</u> relationship problem.

He claims the bad news is that perpetual problems are from basic personality differences that won't go away. The good news is that feeling good about how they interact is more important to the couple than solving the problem.

Why are John Gottman's findings important? Most marriage advisers have a theory and build their advice around their hypotheses, right or wrong. Gottman, instead, studied hundreds of actual couples in real-life settings to see how they interacted. His statements are based on numbers, not nuances.

The three personality types, according to Gottman

In a **Conflict-Avoider** type of marriage, the partners resolve their issues by avoiding or minimizing them. They "agree to disagree." They reaffirm what they love about the marriage, accentuate the positive, and ignore the rest. Gottman has observed that you don't have to talk things out to have a good marriage.

In a **Volatile** style of marriage, the partners express more emotions, both negative and positive. They laugh a lot, are very affectionate, and also can have volcanic arguments. Because they believe that honesty is very important in a marriage, they don't censor their thoughts.

Volatile couples see themselves as equals. They are independent types who believe marriage should strengthen their individuality. Together, they have separate spaces and respect each other's privacy. Their marriage is mainly passionate and exciting.

In a **Validator** type of marriage, the partners, even in the middle of an argument, will take time to validate what the other is saying, even when they don't agree. The man sees himself as analytical, dominant, and assertive, whereas the woman views herself as nurturing, warm and expressive. They probably assume stereotypical roles, where she takes care of the children and the house and he makes the final decisions.

Validating couples tend to be good friends who put the we-ness of the marriage over their individual goals and values.

Now, if I asked you which type of couple would be the happiest, you're apt to choose the Validator. You'd be wrong. The Avoidant? No.

The answer, according to Gottman, is that all three types can be very successful—if both partners are the same type. If they're not, there can be all kinds of problems.

(To see what type couple you are, take the test at the end of this chapter.)

Success is based on a healthy balance of positive and negative emotions.

Gottman states that success is not based on how similar you are in your points of view, marital bliss, perfect compatibility or how often you have sex. (In fact, some marriages may need some negativity and difference to thrive.) The three types can be equally successful if, and this is the important finding, there's a healthy balance between positive and negative feelings and actions.

A healthy balance doesn't mean tit for tat. The healthy ratio of positive to negative interactions is five to one. Yes, for every negative thing you say, you should say five empowering things. This is what will keep a couple stable.

Successful **volatile** types may scream and yell, but they may also have more than five times as many episodes of loving and making up. **Avoidant** types are less critical so they keep the balance at five to one.

The negative actions are criticism; contempt; defensiveness and withdrawal; stonewalling; and isolation. Anger is only a factor if it's expressed **along with** criticism or contempt.

So what does this mean?

How to show positive emotion.

- Show interest. Actually be interested in what your partner is saying.
- Be affectionate. Show you care. Practice small acts of thoughtfulness.
- Be appreciative. Think fondly of your partner and remember contented moments of your life together. When you agree with their ideas and

suggestions, say so. Compliment them and be proud.
- Show concern. Be supportive when your partner is down.
- Be empathic. Understand when they feel something emotionally and convey your understanding of their feelings.
- Joke, tease, be light with each other.

Divorces have a 1.25 to 1 negativity balance. That means for every nice thing you say, you make slightly more comments of a negative nature.

Most relationships follow the same downward negativity spiral. They go from Complaint to Criticism to Contempt to Defensiveness to Stonewalling.

Complaint to contempt: what's the difference?

A **complaint** is specific, about one event. It tells how you feel. "I'm mad because you didn't tell me you'd be late for dinner." Fair enough.

A **criticism** is broader and includes blaming. Often "never" and "always" is part of the criticism. "You never call me when you're late for dinner. You always ruin my evening. You're insensitive!"

Contempt includes accusations of incompetence, doltishness, etc. "You bastard, why can't you get home on time?"

Defensiveness runs rampant when the partner feels they have no part in the argument. "It's not me, it's you." They whine, make excuses, and disengage from any responsibility. They are out of the argument and into protecting themselves. "Me? What did I have to do with ruining your dinner? You know I have to work late to keep food on the table."

Stonewalling occurs when one partner absents himself (85% of stonewallers are men) by emotionally or physically detaching from the argument. They withdraw from any meaningful interaction. They may seem icy and disdainful.

In actuality, men's reaction can be mainly physiological. When men feel threatened, their pulse and heart rate rise alarmingly. They feel like they're swimming in a whirlpool of emotion. Detaching is an attempt to control their feelings of panic, overwhelm, and flooding.

Every relationship will have moments of tension, insensitivity, and disagreement. This is normal. The secret is to know how to communicate so that you are honest and authentic with your partner.

Effective communication
Three-part "I statements."

Be as specific as possible when you complain. Communicate with a Three-part "I-statement."

1. When you (do this)_____
2. I feel_____
3. What I'd like is_____."

An example: 1. "**When you** don't tell me that you're going to be late for dinner, **I feel** like you don't care about my feelings at all and that you don't really like the way I cook. **What I'd like is** for you to call me by noon to let me know your schedule." The secret is to let it be about what you want instead of what a no-good, lousy, son-of-a-gun they are. Which leads us to . . .

"You messages."

A "You message" focuses on the other person's negative actions or statements. It sounds like this: "**You** never call me when you're going to be late" or "**You're** a slob; **you** always leave your dirty clothes on the floor." It automatically puts the other in a defensive position and makes them wrong. Rather, learn to say something like this: "Today I would really appreciate a call from you before 3:00 if you are going to be late." Or "When your dirty clothes are left on the floor, I feel like your slave and like you don't respect me. What can we do about this?"

Don't name call or put-down the other person. Don't tell her what she "should" do. Focus on how you can communicate differently in the relationship and what you want (the **I** part) rather than how your **partner** should change (the **You** part.)

To keep your statement as a complaint rather than a criticism or contempt;
- Remove the blame from your comments
- Say how you **feel**
- Don't criticize your partner's personality
- Don't insult, mock or use sarcasm
- Be direct, not passive-aggressive
- Stick with one situation rather than kitchen-sinking your whole history
- Don't analyze your partner's personality
- Don't mind-read
- Don't threaten or patronize
- Don't condescend
- Don't use "you" messages

Guess what? In good marriages there are complaints and criticism too; there's stonewalling; there's defensiveness. It happens—except for the contempt. The difference is that good marriages repair the damage—and the sooner the better.

Repairing damage.

Gottman says that he best way to repair the damage is to recognize the signs that your partner is becoming upset, hurt, defensive, critical and/or withdrawn and go into a **soothing** mode. There are several methods of soothing:

- Stop the action. Call for a time out. Actually stop all talking and go cool off.
- Edit your responses. Concentrate on the <u>constructive part</u> of your partner's comments and completely ignore the sarcasm, insinuation or criticism that is also there.
- Be a traffic cop. Direct how you want the conversation to go. Phrases like "Go on," "Stop interrupting me," and "I'm not finished," are traffic-cop instructions. And they're okay!
- Stay on focus. Stay on the subject. Don't start kitchen-sinking, i.e., going into the history of every argument you've ever had.
- Use humor. An attempt to lighten up can work wonders.
- Minimize. Realize and state that the argument isn't very important compared to all the good things in the marriage.
- Show affection. Especially when a spouse is flooding with emotion, telling him you love him and really care can help diminish the panic.

Many therapists talk about the Pursuer-Distancer model where one person, usually the man, distances, withdraws to his cave, while the other partner, usually the woman, tries to chase him in there, to keep explaining or attempting to fix what's wrong.

Women, instead of pursuing and demanding an answer from a partner who is flooded, overwhelmed, and stonewalling, attempt to soothe, show affection, and see his point of view.

The cave man is not going to willingly come out if there's a person with a club waiting to attack. He'll come out of his safe place only when the coast seems clear and there is a gentle hand waiting to feed and calm and reassure him. Who can blame him?

The marital hotspots

The two big hotspots in marriages are sex and housework. Men need to realize that women have to feel safe, honored and loved before their libido turns on. Men also need to try to take on more chores. Even men who say they support feminist ideas put in, on average, only forty minutes more housework per day than traditional men who put in next to nothing! Inequities in housework and childcare have profound effects on the marital satisfaction of women.

Expectations

A huge area of contention comes from dealing with the big bag of expectations that each partner hauls into the marriage. What we expect comes mainly from what we experience in our families. Remember all the baggage that goes with children of divorce, alcoholics and dysfunctional families? People enter marriages expecting the positive experiences in their family to be duplicated and the negative ones to be replaced by more positive ones. How realistic is that?

When this doesn't happen, the couple will first feel disappointment. If repair mechanisms don't take place, hurt and/or anger will follow. If the anger continues without repair mechanisms put into place, resentment and eventually bitterness will follow. One or both of the partners will start storing memories in what authors Guerin, Fay, Burden, and Kautto call the "Bitter Bank." When there is too much bitterness, too many unmet expectations, one partner moves across a symbolic bridge to an "island of vulnerability, a state of withdrawal or stonewalling . . . at a place where they cannot be hurt or reached emotionally."

Common unrealistic expectations include:
- My partner and I should feel a deep, unbroken bond at all times
- My partner should be able to anticipate my needs
- I shouldn't have to work for love
- The chemistry is either right or wrong
- My partner should love me unconditionally
- My partner should be emotionally available to me whenever I need them
- A good relationship is free of conflict
- We shouldn't have to work at feeling sexual desire; it should come naturally
- If I'm not happy in my life or relationship, it's my partner's fault
- Living together should be easy

As writer/therapist Judith Viorst says in *Grown-Up Marriage:*

We always ask more of marriage than marriage can give us. We idealize the person we choose to partner with no matter how certain we are that we're seeing clearly. We bring our secret hopes to the relationship. We aren't prepared for the harms we can do to each other. We aren't always aware that love does not preclude hate.

And as Robert Epstein says, in talking about his three pillars for learned love, love victims have the "Happily ever after" syndrome and have no knowledge about the various phases of married life. Instead of just looking to the wedding or thinking that it will always be just like it is today, look to the future. What will marriage be like with children; with the sex-drive greatly diminished; with family duties and careers once more taking front stage?

Managing and having realistic expectations, and looking ahead to what might be bumps in the road and how you might deal with them, is important so that you don't sabotage yourself by living in a fantasy world.

Exercises for getting the love you want.

Harville Hendrix, in *Getting the Love You Want*, designs some practical exercises for Perfect Partnering. Here are two examples:

The Vision exercise.

First, share your vision. How do you do that? Each person writes down his or her personal vision of a deeply satisfying love relationship, stating what they want to keep of what's already there and what they want to add that's missing. The vision is positive and in the present tense, i.e., "We are affectionate with each other." Write down all the things that are important.

Then share your statements. Underline the items you have in common. Feel free to add to your list the partner's statements that you didn't think of but would also like. Now individually rank the items from 1 to 5 in order of importance to you. Combine the statements into "Our Relationship Vision" starting with the "1's." Post it where you'll see it daily.

The Romancing exercise.

On separate pieces of paper write "I feel loved and cared about when you . . . " Make a list. Write what your partner is already doing, and be specific. Then recall when you were first courting. Write a list of "I used to feel loved and cared about when you . . ." Now go beyond that and fantasize. "I would like you to . . ."

Combine your three lists, past, present and future, and rank what you like, scaling from 1 to 5. Exchange your lists. Cross out the ones you're not willing to do, explaining why. Then take the things you are willing to do and start doing them. It's much easier to get what you want when you ask for it, rather than waiting for your partner to somehow magically know what would make you happy.

Relational esteem.

Most of us are never taught how to relate to our partners. One of the most important aspects of our life is left to what we "pick up" from our families of origin, the movies, and past experiences.

Terry Real, director of the Relational Recovery Institute in Cambridge, believes that couples are often destroyed due to cultural norms. Men are still looking for the wife their Dad had. And women, who are making more money, who are financially independent, who can have their own babies, and can function socially as a Single, are expecting more from the men they partner with. They expect them to be equal partners, which means carrying half the load. A vast gender schism exists today.

In order for marriages to work, each sex has to change. Men must learn how to please the women and women must learn how to appreciate the men.

In addition to making these fundamental changes, Dr. Real believes that there are five main steps to learning intimacy and relationship skills.

1. Learn **relational esteem**, which is "the ability to hold your relationship in warm positive regard in spite of its imperfections." Since most relationships have cycles of harmony, disharmony, and repair, we must learn to stay connected even when we are disconnected.

2. **Speak with grace and love.** Dr. Real includes using "I" statements and not using criticism and complaint in his toolbox of skills. He also believes that the question is not "Who's right?" but "How can we solve the problem?"

3. **Listen relationally.** This involves using an internal boundary that lets you listen with detachment, without getting upset, so that you can decide if your partner's statements are true or incorrect. It also involves looking for the

positive, the love, and the helpfulness in the statements.

4. **Contract.** Decide what you want the relationship to look like or how you want any part of it to operate. Remember back when I asked you what commitment looked like to you? This is contracting. It gives behaviorally-defined, specific, measurable goals. If the commitment is made, then breaking it is a boundary violation for the hurt person and a standard's violation for the person breaking the contract.

5. **Practice relational integrity.** This might be the most important part. It is the commitment to stay the course, even in times when your partner wavers.

The key to learning relational skills is to keep the end in mind. The end is not to win the argument or the contest but to repair the break as quickly as possible.

Deciding it's not going to work.

It is my profound hope that you have worked on the issues giving you trouble and been able to correct them so that you foresee the way to future happiness with this partner.

But what if that's not to be? What if you've worked, tried and counseled, and you know in your heart and/or mind that this is not going to be the perfect partner for you? But you've invested from twelve months to two years with this person. You're at that fork in the road where you need to decide whether to hold or fold. What do you do?

You let the partner go. I know how heartbreaking this can be. But what's your choice? To live with someone who will not make you happy for the rest of your life or to find someone who will? Do you really want to be fully committed to this person, to have a child with this person, to create a family of two to three children with this person, and then to have them disappoint you, leave you, or not support you physically, emotionally, or financially?

Be kind to yourself. Let the person go. And then, don't beat up on yourself. Look what you did! You:

1. Entered into a relationship with your eyes open
2. Chose someone based on your values that met your Perfect Partner profile
3. Explored the relationship at a pace that allowed you to get to know the person without first giving away your heart
4. Protected yourself from disappointment and unmet expectations
5. Faced and worked on problems as soon as you knew they were there
6. Went through the necessary steps to overcoming the obstacles

You were superb! You don't deserve to have this heartache happen to you. But sometimes it does.

So what do you do next?

First you cry. You grieve. You get sad. You are disappointed. Then you get mad–but not at yourself. Unless you let down your boundaries.

And then you write down what you learned. And you go back to the beginning of the book. You go through the assessments, altering what you denied, didn't foresee or didn't use which led to becoming involved with someone incompatible.

Don't stop trying! Don't get frustrated with yourself or the dating scene. You know what to do now. Maybe you'll need to make modifications to protect yourself. But you know what they are.

So hold your head up, be really proud of how you went through the whole process, and start over. Instead of crying because it's over, can you smile because it happened?

Copy this card and put it everywhere you can so that you can remind yourself of where you are now.

Although I have just broken up a long-term relationship, I am proud of how I handled the situation and myself. I know I made the right decision for me and for my future. I may have short-time sadness and regret, but I have protected myself from long-term unhappiness. Good for me!

I also know that I am lovable and have the capacity to find and marry my true love. I have the skills and qualities to enter into a relationship that will bring me lasting joy and fulfillment. All I need is to begin.

Marriage has no guarantees. If that's what you're looking for, go live with a car battery.
Erma Bombeck

A *People* Predictor

In the January, 2001 *People*, two couples are spotlighted. One is Liza Minelli and her fiancé, David Gest. The other is Jennifer Aniston and her husband, Brad Pitt.

Pretend you don't know the outcome.

Which pair do you, as almost-seasoned members of the "Finding the Perfect Partner" system, think will have a happy marriage?

With Liza and David, they met just three months ago. It is her fourth walk down the aisle.

What did she like?: "He was attractive." He: "Her eyes."

Did she know he was going to propose? : "I hadn't a clue, because we both discussed how we we're never going to get married."

When asked, she immediately said, "Yes."

Will it work? David: "You know when it's right."

Liza: "I've never had anyone take care of me before."

Hello! This would be laughable if it weren't ultimately so sad, so doomed.

Now let's look at the Pitts.

Says she: "It's very cool when you have your best friend at your side."

Say friends: "They're both funny. They're very, very, much alike. They have the same appreciation for aesthetics, and share a love of antiques. They are the same person, only he's a guy and she's a girl. They totally trust and support each other."

And they're still married!

Blast off!

This is the point where all systems are go. You are happy, committed, and engaged. You have set a date.

The final commitment.

Sometimes before marriage, particular religious denominations will ask the couple they are marrying to attend a counseling weekend, such as "Engaged Encounter." I encourage everyone to seek premarital counseling to discuss four important areas: sex, children, money, and in-laws.

Following is a commitment document that I feel delineates what love and marriage are about. I hope you will use it and enjoy an exciting future with your perfect partner.

The Commitment Document

1. I am entering this relationship with the full understanding of the exciting risks involved and a willingness to give up unrealistic myths, no matter how cherished.

- I understand that nothing is forever, there are no absolute guarantees, and that **now** is the only real forever.
- I understand that ". . . and they lived happily ever after" exists only in fairy tales, and that sustaining romantic love without continuing work, planning and effective interpersonal skill is a myth.

2. I understand that my fulfillment as a person does not ultimately depend upon you nor upon any other person, and that, even though I commit to be with you, I accept my ultimate aloneness and responsibility for myself.

- I cannot make you happy or unhappy, but I can make myself happy.
- My happiness will be an invitation for you to join me in happiness, joy and love.
- I give up the myth that there is a "one and only" who will make me happy.

3. I understand that freedom defined as no commitments or responsibilities is a myth.

- When I make commitments to do what I want to do, then I am being free.
- Freedom to be me and own myself comes from within—not from you or circumstances around me.
- By being responsible I will be free.
- I cannot own another human being nor can I be owned as a possession of another.

4. I understand that there is no absolute equality between standards and characteristics in people who are separate and different; there is equality of rights between people.

- I give up the myth that our relationship cannot have different standards.

- We are separate people with our own standards and they must never be fused into one standard.
- I will feel pride in you and your differences from me.

5. I understand that emotional vulnerability is a myth.

- No one can take away my power, which is my capacity to assert myself to achieve my wishes; no one can control me or make me do anything.
- Power as defined as the capacity of others to manipulate or influence me to do their bidding against my will is a myth.

6. I understand that there will be pain as well as joy, and I accept the risk of a brief period of grief when we part.

7. I will love, honor, respect, but not obey nor subjugate myself to you.

8. I will stay with you during bad times as well as good.

- I will be by your side with caring, kindness, compassion, understanding, consideration and warmth during sickness and natural disaster as well as during health and periods free of disaster.

- I will not be counted on for caring and compassion at repeated times of contrived illness or disaster.
- While I will be strong with you when you feel weak, I expect you likewise to be strong with me when I feel weak.

9. I will accept you as you are, not attack you nor diminish you publicly nor privately, nor push you to change those things that I do not like about you.

- I understand the difference between a role (like husband and wife) and a person. I will not diminish you by thinking of you as "the wife" or "the husband."
- I will cherish you as a unique person.

10. I will give to you for my inner joy, not from duty, without feeling that "I have to" or "you owe me."

11. I will keep my mind healthy, attractive, and lovable.

- Don't expect me to accept you as you are when you fail to maintain mental attractiveness and fail to take care of your mind.
- I will expect you to value your mind.

12. I will ask clearly for whatever I wish from you without feeling that I'm begging, without feeling that I shouldn't have to ask and without assuming that you can read my mind.

- I will put myself first.
- By keeping myself full, satisfied, and not hungry, I will have an abundance of joy, love, and caring to give to you.
- Then, when I give love to you, I am experiencing love for myself.

13. I will not attempt to control or be controlled by money.

- I will own my separate money and property and enjoy sharing ownership with you of my common money and property.
- Since you and I are not children, the concepts of giving and accepting an "allowance," checking up on the other's money spending, and asking permission of the other to spend money is not relevant to our relationship.
- I will share an equal responsibility with you in understanding and planning our mutual finances.

14. I will be reliable so that we will maintain a basis for trust between us.

- I won't say that I will do anything unless I truly want to and unless I actually will.
- While I accept the right to have private areas of my life that I will not share with you, I will not sneak on you, nor will I lie to you by either active commission or by failure to share relevant information that affects our relationship.

15. I will respect, accept and appreciate your saying **no**.

- I understand that only by our mutual acceptance of no will we both be able to say yes and mean it fully.
- While I accept my momentary human response of frustration with disappointment, I will not act rejected, will not sulk nor continue to be hurt or angry; nor will I attempt to control your expression of your individuality in any way.

16. I will accept your bad feelings of anger, sadness, helplessness and fear as well as joy.

- I will listen to your expressions of frustration without taking your feelings as a personal attack and without trying to control your expressions of feeling in any way.
- I will not harbor grudges nor keep vengeful feelings.
- I will start a good quarrel in which we both win whenever I experience bad feelings that may interfere with our closeness and love.
- When I feel bad, I will come to you face-to-face with my feelings.
- No matter how angry or upset I get, I will never threaten to nor actually harm you physically; I will never threaten to nor actually abandon you, "drop out" or "go crazy."

17. While I will not accept responsibility for your feelings or behavior, I will accept my responsibility to myself for whatever I do with you.

- I understand that in your love you have exposed your human weaknesses.
- I will never ridicule, tease you or use vengefully what you have trusted me to know about you.

18. I will leave the past behind. I will henceforth resolve all bad feelings about my past mistakes and never bring them up to you.

- I understand that being sorry for my past mistakes does not help you or me now, so I will give up any sorrow that I feel for past mistakes.
- I will give up wishing that anything in the past was different because, no matter how much I wish, my wishing will not change it now.
- While I will learn from the past, I will not live in it.
- I will experience being with you **now** while sharing hopes, dreams and plans for the future.

19. Since I understand that we cannot be everything to each other, I will respect and value the importance of your having separate play and work activities with separate friends and coworkers.

- There are limits with which I will not feel OK.
- I will be aware of my limits of acceptance and let you know clearly.
- I will respect your confidences and never share with another those things that you share with me privately without obtaining your agreement in advance.
- I will keep this commitment even should we part.

20. I will place high priority and value on our fun together.

- I understand that for us to want to stay together and be free of boredom, I must share enthusiasm and responsiveness.
- So, I will consistently enjoy sharing those parts of myself which you enjoy.

21. I will value and protect my sexual expression of sharing fun and love.

Marsha Wayne

The Relationship-Style Questionnaire
From John Gottman

1. I will often hide my feelings to avoid hurting my spouse.
   You: *YES*   *NO*
   Partner: *YES*   *NO*

2. When I disagree, I often solve the problem by going back to my basic beliefs about the different roles of men and women.
   You: *YES*   *NO*
   Partner: *YES*   *NO*

3. When I disagree, I don't believe there is much point in analyzing my feelings and motivations.
   You: *YES*   *NO*
   Partner: *YES*   *NO*

4. I have a lot of separate friends.
   You: *YES*   *NO*
   Partner: *YES*   *NO*

5. It is important to attend a church or synagogue regularly.
   You: *YES*   *NO*
   Partner: *YES*   *NO*

6. Many marriage conflicts are solved just through passing of time.
   You: *YES*   *NO*
   Partner: *YES*   *NO*

7. We each do a lot of things on our own.
   You: *YES*   *NO*
   Partner: *YES*   *NO*

8. During a marital conflict, there is not much to be gained from figuring out what is happening on a psychological level.
   You: *YES*   *NO*
   Partner: *YES*   *NO*

9. My religious values give me a clear sense of life's purposes.
   You: *YES*   *NO*
   Partner: *YES*   *NO*

10. When I'm moody I prefer to be left alone until I get over it.
    You: *YES*   *NO*
    Partner: *YES*   *NO*

11. I don't feel very comfortable with strong displays of negative emotion in our marriage.
    You: *YES*   *NO*
    Partner: *YES*   *NO*

12. I turn to my basic religious or cultural values for guidance when resolving conflicts.
    You: *YES*   *NO*
    Partner: *YES*   *NO*

13. I just accept most of the things in my marriage that I can't change.
    You: *YES*   *NO*
    Partner: *YES*   *NO*

14. We often agree not to talk about things we disagree about.

    You: *YES*   *NO*
    Partner: *YES*   *NO*

15. In our marriage there is a fairly clear line between the husband's and the wife's roles.

    You: *YES*   *NO*
    Partner: *YES*   *NO*

16. We just don't seem to disagree very much.

    You: *YES*   *NO*
    Partner: *YES*   *NO*

17. When we have some difference of opinion we often drop the topic.

    You: *YES*   *NO*
    Partner: *YES*   *NO*

18. We hardly ever have much to argue about.

    You: *YES*   *NO*
    Partner: *YES*   *NO*

19. A lot of talking about disagreements often makes matters worse.

    You: *YES*   *NO*
    Partner: *YES*   *NO*

20. There are some personal areas in my life that I prefer not to discuss with my spouse.

    You: *YES*   *NO*
    Partner: *YES*   *NO*

21. There is not much point in trying to persuade my partner of my viewpoint.
    You: *YES*   *NO*
    Partner: *YES*   *NO*

22. There's not much to be gained by getting openly angry with my spouse.
    You: *YES*   *NO*
    Partner: *YES*   *NO*

23. Thinking positively solves a lot of marital issues.
    You: *YES*   *NO*
    Partner: *YES*   *NO*

24. In marriage it is usually best to stick to the traditional values about men and women.
    You: *YES*   *NO*
    Partner: *YES*   *NO*

25. I prefer to work out many of my negative feelings on my own.
    You: *YES*   *NO*
    Partner: *YES*   *NO*

26. Going over a lot of negative feelings in a marital discussion usually makes things worse.
    You: *YES*   *NO*
    Partner: *YES*   *NO*

27. If you just relax about problems, they have a way of working themselves out.
    You: *YES*   *NO*
    Partner: *YES*   *NO*

28. When I talk about my problems I find they just aren't that important in the overall picture of my marriage.

You:	YES	NO
Partner:	YES	NO

29. Men and women ought to have separate roles in a marriage.

You:	YES	NO
Partner:	YES	NO

Total the numbers you checked Yes. If the score is 8 or above, you probably have a **conflict-avoider marriage philosophy.** Continue.

1. I think it's a good idea for my partner and me to have a lot of separate friends.

You:	YES	NO
Partner:	YES	NO

2. I believe in honestly confronting disagreements, whatever the issue.

You:	YES	NO
Partner:	YES	NO

3. We often do things separately.

You:	YES	NO
Partner:	YES	NO

4. The feeling of togetherness is very central to our marriage.
   You: *YES*   *NO*
   Partner: *YES*   *NO*

5. Marriage partners should be direct and honest no matter what the results.
   You: *YES*   *NO*
   Partner: *YES*   *NO*

6. I feel quite comfortable with a strong expression of negative feelings.
   You: *YES*   *NO*
   Partner: *YES*   *NO*

7. Sometimes I enjoy a good argument with my spouse.
   You: *YES*   *NO*
   Partner: *YES*   *NO*

8. The most important aspect of marriage is companionship.
   You: *YES*   *NO*
   Partner: *YES*   *NO*

9. Jealousy is sometimes an issue in my marriage.
   You: *YES*   *NO*
   Partner: *YES*   *NO*

10. It is important to be a separate individual in a marriage.
    You: *YES*   *NO*
    Partner: *YES*   *NO*

11. I think we should argue but only about important matters.
    You: *YES*   *NO*
    Partner: *YES*   *NO*

12. We often eat separately.
    You: *YES*   *NO*
    Partner: *YES*   *NO*

13. Our marriage is based on being one another's best friend.
    You: *YES*   *NO*
    Partner: *YES*   *NO*

14. I enjoy being able to persuade my spouse when we have a disagreement.
    You: *YES*   *NO*
    Partner: *YES*   *NO*

15. The religious and other beliefs we share are basic in our marriage.
    You: *YES*   *NO*
    Partner: *YES*   *NO*

16. We believe in keeping our marriage very romantic.
    You: *YES*   *NO*
    Partner: *YES*   *NO*

17. We often look back at our photo albums together.
    You: *YES*   *NO*
    Partner: *YES*   *NO*

18. We cultivate a sense of we-ness in our marriage.
    You: *YES*   *NO*
    Partner: *YES*   *NO*

19. We share all things personal and emotional in our marriage.
    You: *YES*   *NO*
    Partner: *YES*   *NO*

20. All the spaces in our home are shared spaces.
    You: *YES*   *NO*
    Partner: *YES*   *NO*

21. I would never take a vacation separately from my spouse.
    You: *YES*   *NO*
    Partner: *YES*   *NO*

22. At times I enjoy expressing anger.
    You: *YES*   *NO*
    Partner: *YES*   *NO*

23. I believe it is important to fight even about small matters.
    You: *YES*   *NO*
    Partner: *YES*   *NO*

24. I enjoy working out my values through arguments.
    You: *YES*   *NO*
    Partner: *YES*   *NO*

25. There is nothing personal that I do not share with my spouse.
    You: *YES*   *NO*
    Partner: *YES*   *NO*

26. I am comfortable with a moderate amount of emotional expression.
    You: *YES*   *NO*
    Partner: *YES*   *NO*

27. It is essential to have a strong sense of togetherness in marriage.
    You: *YES*   *NO*
    Partner: *YES*   *NO*

28. Keeping a certain amount of distance in a marriage helps the romance.
    You: *YES*   *NO*
    Partner: *YES*   *NO*

29. A strong sense of traditional values is good for a marriage.
    You: *YES*   *NO*
    Partner: *YES*   *NO*

30. There are few issues in a marriage worth arguing about.
    You: *YES*   *NO*
    Partner: *YES*   *NO*

Total scores for numbers 1, 2, 3, 5, 6, 7, 9, 10, 12, 14, 16, 22, 23, 24, and 28. High scores on these questions indicated that you are most comfortable with a "**Volatile**" philosophy of marriage.

Total scores for numbers 4, 8, 11, 13, 15, 17, 18, 19, 20, 21, 25, 26, 27, 29 and 30. High scores on these questions indicate that you are most comfortable with a "**Validator**" philosophy of marriage.

How do I love thee? Let me count the ways.
I love thee to the depth and breadth and height
My soul can reach when feeling out of sight
For the ends of Being and ideal Grace.
I love thee to the level of everyday's
Most quiet need, by sun and candlelight.
I love thee freely, as men strive for Right.
I love thee purely, as they turn from Praise.
I love thee with the passion put to use
In my old griefs, and with my childhood's faith.
I love thee with a love I seemed to lose
With my lost saints,–I love thee with the breath,
Smiles, tears, of all my life! –and, if God choose,
I shall but love thee better after death.

Elizabeth Barrett Browning

In Conclusion.

Dear Reader,

My wish for you is that having read this book to the end you will know:

- How to find single people that are worthy of you
- How to protect yourself from giving your heart and showing your vulnerable areas too soon
- How to deal with rejection without becoming depressed or down on yourself
- How to use information as feedback to improve yourself and/or future relationships
- How to recognize red flags and make wise choices
- What your values, partner profile, boundaries and standards are
- When to hold 'em and when to fold 'em
- How to create a sustained, monogamous, loving relationship
- How to overcome obstacles tossed your way
- How to listen, communicate and "chunk it down"
- How to resolve difficulties that will inevitably appear

And my most fervent desire is that you will find wonderful, enduring, exciting, nurturing **love**, with a marriage partner that is perfect for you in every way.

Marsha Wayne

Bibliography

Authentic Happiness, Martin Seligman.

The Evaluation and Treatment of Marital Conflict, Philip J. Guerin, Jr., Leo F. Fay, Susan L. Burden, Judith Gilbert Kautto.

Date . . . Or Soul Mate?, Neil Clark Warren.

Engaged to marry, eventually. *Conde Nast Bridal Infobank*, as reported in *USA Today*, December 31, 2003.

Falling in Love by Design, *USA Today*, June 26, 2003.

Falling in Love, Why We Choose the Lovers We Choose, Ayala Malach Pines.

Fear of Falling, by Judith Wallerstein, Julia Lewis and Sandra Blakeslee, *Time,* September 25, 2000.

Free Advice, Amy Alkon, Caroline Johnson, Marlol Minnick.

Get Smart about Modern Romantic Relationships, Michelle L. Castro.

Getting the Love you Want, Harville Hendrix.

Grown-Up Marriage, Judith Viorst.

How Can I get Through to You?, Terry Real.

How Not to Stay Single, Nita Tucker with Randi Moret.

How to Make People Like You in 90 Seconds or Less, Nicholas Boothman, *Bottom Line Personal*, 4/1/2003.

If . . . Questions for the Game of Life, Evelyn McFarlane & James Saywell

Love.com, *U.S. News & World Report*, September 29, 2003, quoting Barbara Dafoe Whitehead.

Love Warps the Mind A Little, John Dufresne.

Lovers are Special, Lucy Mead. Source of most of the footnoted quotes.

The 44 Rules, **E. Jean's Guide to a Brilliant Life**, *Elle*.

The Marriage Plan, Aggie Jordan.

Marry Me, Bradley Gerstman, Christopher Pizzo, and Rich Seldes.

Peter Pan, J.M. Barrie.

Ready for Marriage Assessment, the Morbrook Institute.

Seat of the Soul, Gary Zukav.

The Road Not Taken, Robert Frost.

Stress Detracts from Sex Life, *USA Today*, November 12, 2001.

That Old Feeling, *Time,* February 2002.

Why Marriages Succeed or Fail, John Gottman.

Speeches:

Leo Buscaglia, From a Tony Robbins "Powertalk!" Tape

John Gottman, Victoria Theater, Santa Barbara,

Marsha Wayne

Fall, 1999.

Terry Real, Relational Renewal Training for Therapists, Cambridge, Massachusetts, September, 2003.

Marianne Williamson, Arlington Theater, Santa Barbara, Spring. 2001.

About the Author

Marsha Wayne is a personal and small business coach and president of Wayne & Wayne–Coaching for Success. She teaches classes at Adult Ed on relationships and careers and hosts a weekly radio show, *Call the Coach*.

She has an MBA from Harvard Business School and has specialized in marketing and long-range planning, both invaluable tools when it comes to finding your true love.

In addition, she holds a Masters in clinical psychology and has worked with many couples in counseling.

Wayne learned about dating, rating and mating from personal experience, her clients, and, then again, by having four daughters.

She lives in Santa Barbara, California with her first husband.

To Reach Marsha

Marsha Wayne
can be reached at
(805) 564-6075

e-mail:
marshawayne@cox.net

FAX:(805) 969-0121

website: www.marshawayne.com

I also offer this in teleclass form and as a 4-hour seminar.

Check for more information at
www.marshawayne.com